The Full Moon's Curse

Lila Frost

Published by Bright Minds Books, 2024.

While every precaution has been taken in the preparation of this book, the publisher assumes no responsibility for errors or omissions, or for damages resulting from the use of the information contained herein.

THE FULL MOON'S CURSE

First edition. October 5, 2024.

Copyright © 2024 Lila Frost.

ISBN: 979-8227433237

Written by Lila Frost.

Table of Contents

Description

In the quiet town of Hollowdale, a powerful curse haunts the land, tied to the full moon and a mysterious magic hidden deep within the earth.

Emma and her friends—Liam, Mia, and Noah—are thrust into a thrilling adventure as they unravel the secrets of the ancient magic that has controlled their town for centuries.Facing trials of fire, water, and their own deepest fears, they must learn to balance the power of the magic while protecting their home from those who would misuse it.

The Full Moon's Curse is a tale of courage, friendship, and the responsibility that comes with power.

Dedication

To all the dreamers who face their fears and embrace the magic within. This story is for those who believe that the greatest adventures come from stepping into the unknown, and that true strength comes from the bonds we share with the people who stand by our side.

Preface

Every town has its secrets, but some secrets are more powerful—and more dangerous—than others. In Hollowdale, the legend of an ancient curse has been passed down for generations, whispered during full moons and quiet nights.

But what happens when the curse isn't just a story? **The Full Moon's Curse** began as an exploration of the idea that magic, like life, is a force that requires balance, understanding, and respect.

This story follows a group of friends who face impossible challenges, both physical and emotional, and learn that true power lies not in control, but in connection.

Chapter 1: The Night of the Full Moon

It was Halloween night in the small town of Hollowdale, and the streets were alive with excitement. The houses were decorated with glowing pumpkins, spooky ghosts, and fake cobwebs, as children in costumes raced from house to house collecting candy. Among the crowd were four friends—Emma, Liam, Mia, and Noah—dressed in their own Halloween outfits, ready for a night of fun.

As the evening went on, the group wandered to the outskirts of town, where the woods loomed dark and mysterious. Hollowdale had a legend about these woods, passed down through generations. It was said that on the night of a full moon, strange and eerie things happened. But like most legends, the kids didn't take it seriously. After all, it was just a story, right?

Emma, dressed as a vampire with a long black cape, looked up at the sky and noticed something strange. The full moon was brighter than she had ever seen, casting an almost eerie glow over the woods. She nudged her friends, pointing it out.

"Look at the moon! It's so bright tonight," she said.

Liam, who was dressed as a werewolf, grinned. "Perfect for a spooky adventure, don't you think? Let's go check out the woods."

Mia, the cautious one of the group, hesitated. "I don't know, guys. It's Halloween night, and the woods are always creepy. Plus, with that old legend—"

"Oh, come on, Mia," Noah interrupted. He was the bravest of the group, dressed as a superhero, complete with a cape and mask. "It's just a silly story. Nothing's going to happen."

The group exchanged glances, and despite Mia's reluctance, curiosity won out. They made their way toward the edge of the woods, feeling the crisp autumn air grow colder as they approached.

As they stepped into the forest, the sound of the bustling town faded away, leaving only the rustling of leaves and the occasional hoot of an owl. The woods were darker than they expected, with the tall trees blocking much of the moonlight. Emma pulled her cape tighter around her shoulders, feeling a shiver that wasn't just from the cold.

Suddenly, a long, eerie howl echoed through the trees. The sound was so chilling that it stopped the friends in their tracks.

"Did you hear that?" Mia whispered, her voice shaky.

The group stood frozen, listening. The howl came again, this time louder and closer. It was followed by another sound—one that sent a chill down their spines. It was their names, being called softly but clearly.

"Emma... Liam... Mia... Noah..."

They all heard it. They looked at each other, eyes wide with fear. Who was calling them? And how did they know their names?

"We should go," Mia whispered, taking a step back. "Now."

Before anyone could argue, the trees around them seemed to sway unnaturally, as if alive. A shadowy figure appeared in the distance, standing still but watching them intently. The figure was too far away to make out clearly, but its presence was enough to send the group into a panic.

Without another word, they turned and ran back toward the town as fast as their legs could carry them. The sounds of the woods seemed to close in around them—branches snapping, leaves crunching underfoot, and that eerie howling growing louder.

Finally, they burst out of the woods and onto the lit streets of Hollowdale. The sight of the familiar houses and the laughter of trick-or-treaters brought a wave of relief. They stopped to catch their breath, hearts pounding.

Lessons from Chapter 1: The Night of the Full Moon

1. **Curiosity can lead to unexpected adventures**: The friends' decision to explore the woods, despite the spooky legend, led them to an encounter they never expected. Sometimes

curiosity opens the door to new experiences.

2. **Trust your instincts**: Mia's hesitation about going into the woods was a sign that something wasn't right. Trusting your instincts can help you avoid trouble.

3. **The unknown can be frightening**: The group learned that stepping into the unknown, like the dark woods, can be scary. But it's also part of every adventure.

4. **It's okay to be afraid**: Even the bravest of the group, Noah, felt fear when faced with something mysterious. Being afraid doesn't make you weak.

5. **Stick together with friends**: The friends stayed together when they were scared, which helped them face the unknown as a team. Sticking together in difficult times makes challenges easier to face.

Chapter 2: The Mysterious Howl

The night after their eerie adventure in the woods, the friends couldn't stop thinking about what had happened. In school the next day, they gathered around the lunch table, their voices hushed.

"I still can't believe we heard our names in the woods," Mia said, her eyes wide with fear.

"Do you think someone was playing a prank on us?" Noah asked, though even he didn't seem convinced. "Maybe some older kids were trying to scare us."

Liam shook his head. "I don't think it was a prank. It felt... different. And that howling—it wasn't just a dog or anything. It sounded almost like it was calling to us."

Emma, who had been unusually quiet, finally spoke up. "I think we should go back."

The other three stared at her in disbelief.

"Are you serious?" Mia asked, her voice rising. "After what happened last night?"

Emma nodded, her expression determined. "I know it sounds crazy, but I feel like there's something we're supposed to find out. We ran away before we could figure out what was really happening."

"I'm with Emma," Liam said. "If we don't go back, we'll never know. What if it's something important?"

Mia and Noah exchanged nervous glances. They knew their friends had a point. The mystery of the woods had a strange pull, one they couldn't seem to shake.

"Fine," Noah said, sighing. "But we go right after school. No waiting until it's dark."

Mia reluctantly agreed, and the four friends made their plan. As soon as the final bell rang, they gathered their backpacks and met at the edge of the woods. The full moon wouldn't rise until later, but the woods still had an eerie presence, even in the fading daylight.

They hesitated for a moment at the tree line, the events of the previous night still fresh in their minds.

"Are we really doing this?" Mia asked, her voice barely a whisper.

"We have to," Emma replied. She took the first step into the woods, and one by one, the others followed.

The deeper they went, the quieter the world around them became. The cheerful sounds of the town faded, replaced by the rustling of leaves and the distant caw of crows. It was as if the woods had swallowed them up, trapping them in a world apart from their familiar town.

As they walked, they retraced their steps from the night before, following the same path they had taken when they first heard the howling. Every shadow seemed to move, and every branch seemed to reach out to them. But this time, there was no howling. Just an unsettling silence.

"Maybe it was nothing after all," Noah muttered, kicking at a rock. "Just our imaginations running wild."

But just as the words left his mouth, Emma stopped suddenly. "Wait," she said, pointing to the ground. "Look."

Lying in the middle of the path was something shiny, half-buried in the dirt. It caught the last bit of sunlight filtering through the trees, glinting in a way that made it impossible to miss. Emma knelt down and carefully brushed away the dirt to reveal a silver pendant on a delicate chain.

"Whoa," Liam said, crouching beside her. "What is that?"

"It looks old," Emma whispered. She picked it up, turning it over in her hand. On the back of the pendant, strange symbols were etched into the silver, symbols none of them recognized.

"Do you think it's connected to the howling?" Mia asked, looking around nervously. The pendant gave her an uneasy feeling.

"Maybe," Emma said, standing up. "But why would something like this be out here, in the middle of the woods?"

Liam took the pendant from Emma and examined it. "It's probably part of some old story or something. Maybe a piece of history from the town. Hollowdale's been around forever."

"Or," Noah said with a grin, "it's cursed."

Mia shuddered. "Not funny, Noah."

Emma, however, didn't laugh. The pendant felt strangely warm in her hand, and as she held it, she could almost feel it pulse with energy. It was as if it was alive, as if it was connected to something deeper and more mysterious than any of them could understand.

Lessons from Chapter 2: The Mysterious Howl

1. **Teamwork is important when facing the unknown**: Even though Mia and Noah were scared, they agreed to support Emma and Liam's decision to return to the woods, showing that working together can help overcome fear.

2. **Curiosity can lead to discovery**: Emma's curiosity about the strange events pushed the group to investigate, leading them to find the mysterious pendant. Exploring mysteries often leads to learning new things.

3. **Trust your feelings**: The pendant made Emma feel something special, and trusting her instincts led the group to their next clue. Sometimes, feelings can guide you in the right direction.

4. **Be open to possibilities**: Noah joked about the pendant being cursed, but strange things do happen. Being open-minded can help you prepare for the unexpected.

5. **History holds answers**: The group's decision to research the pendant shows that sometimes the past holds the key to solving present-day mysteries. Looking back can help us understand what's happening now.

Chapter 3: The Secret in the Pendant

The next day, Emma couldn't stop thinking about the pendant. She had kept it hidden under her pillow all night, but strange dreams had haunted her sleep. In one dream, she was running through the woods under the light of a full moon, her feet barely touching the ground as she sped through the trees. She could hear howling in the distance, but it didn't scare her—instead, it felt like the howls were calling her, guiding her somewhere.

When she woke up, she knew that the pendant was more than just a piece of lost jewelry.

After school, the group gathered at Hollowdale's tiny library. It wasn't a place they visited often, but it was the best place to research anything related to the town's history. Miss Duncan, the elderly librarian, greeted them with a smile as they walked in.

"What brings you kids in here today?" she asked, adjusting her glasses.

"We're looking for old books," Emma explained, "about Hollowdale's history. And maybe anything on curses or old legends."

Miss Duncan raised an eyebrow. "Curses, huh? What sort of trouble are you getting into?" she asked, half-joking.

"It's more like... solving a mystery," Liam said, glancing at Emma. They hadn't told Miss Duncan about the pendant, but they knew they needed answers.

"Well, you're in luck," Miss Duncan said, leading them to a corner of the library filled with dusty old books. "This section has all the town's history. You might even find some local legends in there."

The group spent the next hour poring over books, flipping through pages filled with old photographs, maps, and stories about Hollowdale. It was Mia who found something interesting.

"Look at this," she said, pulling a book titled *Tales of Hollowdale: Legends and Mysteries* off the shelf. She opened to a page with an old sketch of a pendant—almost identical to the one Emma had found.

"That's it!" Emma gasped. "That's the pendant!"

The caption below the drawing read: *The Silver Pendant of the Hollow Wolves.*

Liam read aloud from the book: "According to local legend, the Silver Pendant of the Hollow Wolves was crafted centuries ago by a powerful family that lived in the heart of Hollowdale. It is said that the pendant holds a curse—a curse that transforms the wearer into a wolf under the light of the full moon."

"A wolf?" Noah echoed, looking up from his own book. "Like a werewolf?"

Mia's eyes widened. "That's just a story, right?"

Emma shook her head, her fingers gripping the pendant that now hung around her neck. "I don't think it's just a story."

The group continued reading, discovering more about the curse. The legend said that the pendant had once belonged to a family known as the Silvers, who were rumored to have mystical powers tied to the moon. When their land was taken from them, they placed a curse on the pendant, vowing that whoever found it would become a creature of the night.

"The curse can only be broken," Liam read, "if the pendant is returned to its rightful owner, or if the wearer completes a series of three challenges before the next full moon."

"What kind of challenges?" Noah asked, leaning in.

The book didn't say.

"Well, this is getting interesting," Liam said, sitting back. "So, Emma... you might be cursed."

Emma looked down at the pendant, her heart racing. The idea of being cursed seemed impossible, but then again, nothing about the last few days had been normal.

"What if we return it?" Mia suggested. "To whoever it belongs to?"

"But the Silvers don't live here anymore," Noah pointed out. "Their family disappeared a long time ago."

"Which means," Emma said slowly, "we have to complete the challenges."

The group was quiet for a moment, the weight of the situation sinking in. If the legend was true, they had only a short time to break the curse before the next full moon, which was just a few weeks away.

"What happens if you don't complete the challenges?" Mia asked, her voice barely above a whisper.

Liam scanned the page, then closed the book with a grim expression. "It doesn't say. But I don't think we want to find out."

Later that evening, Emma couldn't shake the feeling that something had already started to change. Her senses were sharper—she could hear the faintest rustling of leaves outside her window, and when she stepped outside to get some air, she could smell the damp earth and trees as if they were right in front of her.

Lessons from Chapter 3: The Secret in the Pendant

1. **Knowledge is powerful and can guide you through difficult situations**: The group learned more about the curse and its history by researching in the library, showing that gathering information is the first step in solving any problem.
2. **Sometimes legends hold truths**: The children initially thought the story of the cursed pendant was just a myth, but they soon realized that old stories often have real elements. It's important to keep an open mind.
3. **Taking responsibility for your actions**: Emma found the pendant and recognized that she might be affected by the curse. Instead of running away from the problem, she took responsibility and decided to find a way to break the curse.
4. **Challenges can lead to growth**: Even though the idea of

facing three unknown challenges was scary, the group understood that overcoming them was the only way forward. Facing challenges helps us grow stronger.

5. **Trust your instincts**: Emma's heightened senses and strange dreams were signs that something was changing, and she trusted those instincts to guide her in solving the mystery of the curse.

Chapter 4: The Curse of the Wolves

The weight of the curse hung heavy over the group. Emma could feel it even more—an unsettling change in herself, a connection to something primal and wild that she didn't fully understand. Her senses were sharper, her reactions quicker, and at times, she felt almost like she wasn't entirely herself.

Liam, Noah, and Mia met at Emma's house after school. The full moon was still a couple of weeks away, but they all knew they didn't have much time to break the curse. The question was: how?

"We need to figure out what the first challenge is," Liam said, pacing in Emma's living room. He was always the one to take charge when things got serious. "The book didn't say anything about where to start."

Emma looked down at the pendant around her neck, the silver glinting in the sunlight streaming through the window. "I think the pendant will lead us," she said quietly. "Last night, I had a dream. There was a path in the woods—it felt like it was calling to me."

"You think it's a sign?" Noah asked, raising an eyebrow.

Emma nodded. "I don't know how I know, but I feel it. The first challenge is in the woods."

Mia shivered. "The woods again? We barely made it out last time."

"We don't have a choice," Emma said, standing up. "If we don't do this, I could turn into... something else."

The room fell silent. None of them wanted to say it out loud, but they all knew what the curse meant. If Emma didn't break it, she could turn into a wolf under the next full moon.

"Let's go," Liam said. "The sooner we start, the better."

The four friends made their way to the woods once again, this time with a sense of urgency. As they entered the forest, Emma felt a strange pull, like the trees themselves were guiding her. She followed the feeling, leading the group deeper into the heart of the woods.

The air grew colder, and the shadows longer as they walked. Emma's senses were on high alert—she could hear every rustle of leaves, smell the dampness of the earth, and feel the faintest shifts in the wind. It was almost overwhelming, but she kept moving forward.

Suddenly, they came to a clearing. In the center of the clearing stood an old, gnarled tree, its branches twisted and reaching toward the sky like skeletal hands. The tree looked ancient, like it had been there for centuries, watching over the forest.

"This is it," Emma whispered. "The first challenge."

Liam stepped forward cautiously. "What do we have to do?"

As if in answer, the ground beneath the tree began to glow faintly, revealing a circular stone embedded in the earth. Strange symbols, similar to the ones on Emma's pendant, were etched into the stone.

Noah knelt down to examine the stone. "It's some kind of riddle," he said, pointing to the symbols. "But I can't read it."

Emma's pendant grew warm against her chest, and she instinctively touched it. As she did, the symbols on the stone shifted, rearranging themselves into words they could understand.

"The first challenge is one of strength," Emma read aloud. "To break the curse, you must prove that even in the face of fear, you can stand strong."

Liam looked around, puzzled. "But how do we prove that?"

As if in response, the wind picked up, and a low growl echoed through the trees. The group turned, their eyes widening as shapes emerged from the shadows—wolves, large and menacing, their eyes glowing in the dim light. There were five of them, slowly circling the clearing, their growls growing louder with each step.

Mia gasped, taking a step back. "Wolves..."

Emma's heart pounded in her chest, but she forced herself to stay calm. The pendant around her neck pulsed again, and she realized something: these wolves weren't just ordinary animals. They were part of the challenge, part of the curse.

"We have to stand our ground," she said, her voice steady. "That's what the riddle means. We can't run. We have to prove that we're strong."

"Are you serious?" Noah asked, his eyes wide with fear. "There's no way we can fight them!"

"We're not supposed to fight them," Emma said, her eyes locked on the wolves. "We just have to face them."

The wolves continued to circle, their growls vibrating through the air. Emma could feel the fear building inside her, but she pushed it down, forcing herself to stay rooted in place. She reached out and grabbed Mia's hand, giving it a reassuring squeeze. "We can do this."

One by one, the others followed Emma's lead. Liam stood next to her, fists clenched but his eyes determined. Noah took a deep breath and joined them, standing firm despite the fear in his eyes. Mia, though shaking, held her ground.

The wolves came closer, their breath hot on the air. For a moment, it seemed like they were going to attack. But then, just as they reached the edge of the clearing, they stopped. Their glowing eyes locked onto the group, but they made no move to pounce.

Emma's pendant glowed brighter, and she felt a sense of calm wash over her. The wolves watched them for a long moment, then, one by one, they turned and disappeared back into the shadows.

The group stood there, stunned, their hearts still racing.

Lessons from Chapter 4: The Curse of the Wolves

1. **Sometimes, what seems fun at first can have serious consequences**: The adventure in the woods started out as fun, but the group learned that there are real consequences, especially when facing something dangerous like a curse.
2. **Facing fear is part of being strong**: The challenge in the woods wasn't about fighting the wolves; it was about standing strong and facing their fear without running away.

3. **Courage comes in many forms**: Even though Mia was scared, she stayed with her friends and faced the wolves. Courage isn't the absence of fear, but the decision to act despite it.

4. **Teamwork makes you stronger**: By standing together, the group was able to face the challenge. Each person's strength helped the others overcome their fear.

5. **Challenges help us grow**: The group learned that facing challenges head-on, even when they're scary, helps them grow stronger. Challenges are opportunities to prove what we're capable of.

Chapter 5: The Old Witch's Warning

The group barely had time to catch their breath after the encounter with the wolves before Emma's pendant glowed again. This time, it pulsed more intensely, the warm light flickering like a heartbeat. Everyone gathered around her, staring at the pendant.

"That was just the first challenge," Emma said softly, still feeling the energy of the pendant. "We have two more to go."

"But how are we supposed to know what the next challenge is?" Mia asked, her voice still shaky from the recent encounter. "Are we supposed to wait for another pack of wolves to show up?"

Liam frowned, thinking. "The riddle we solved talked about strength. Maybe the next challenge is about something else. But we need more clues."

Noah nodded, agreeing with Liam. "Maybe the pendant will tell us again, like it did with the wolves. But I don't know if we have time to wait. What if the full moon comes before we figure out the last two challenges?"

Emma looked around the darkening woods. The trees swayed lightly in the evening breeze, and she could hear the distant howls of wolves far off in the distance. The night was still young, but there was a sense of urgency building inside her.

"We need help," Emma said finally. "Someone who knows more about this curse than we do."

"Who?" Mia asked. "No one in town even believes in this stuff."

Liam suddenly snapped his fingers. "Wait! What about Old Agnes?"

Old Agnes was the town's recluse. Some people called her a witch, while others just thought of her as a strange old lady who lived on the outskirts of Hollowdale. She rarely came into town, and when she did, people whispered about her. But there were always rumors that Agnes knew things—things that others didn't.

"You think she'll help us?" Noah asked, raising an eyebrow.

"She has to know something," Liam insisted. "If she's lived here her whole life, she's bound to know about the town's legends. Maybe she even knows something about the pendant or the curse."

Emma hesitated for a moment. She had heard all kinds of stories about Old Agnes—stories that made her a little nervous about visiting the woman. But they didn't have any other options, and time was running out.

"Okay," Emma said, nodding. "Let's go see her."

Old Agnes lived in a small, weathered house on the far edge of Hollowdale. The house was surrounded by a wild garden, overgrown with vines and strange plants that twisted and curled in every direction. A tall, crooked fence made of gnarled wood encircled the property, and the gate creaked loudly as the group pushed it open.

"I don't like this," Mia whispered as they approached the front door. "It's too spooky."

Noah gave her a playful nudge. "Come on, Mia. She's probably just a regular old lady. No need to be scared."

Liam knocked on the door, and for a moment, there was no answer. Then, slowly, the door creaked open, revealing a tall, thin woman with wild gray hair and sharp eyes that gleamed like she could see straight through them. She was dressed in a long, tattered cloak, and around her neck hung several strange amulets.

"You've come," Agnes said, her voice low and raspy. "I've been expecting you."

Emma and her friends exchanged glances. How could she have been expecting them?

"Come in," Agnes said, opening the door wider. "There's much to discuss."

The group hesitantly stepped into her house. The interior was just as strange as the exterior—shelves filled with jars of herbs, dried flowers hanging from the ceiling, and a large fireplace that cast flickering shadows across the room. In the center of the room was a small wooden table, where Agnes motioned for them to sit.

"You're here about the pendant," Agnes said, sitting down across from them. Her eyes flicked to the glowing pendant around Emma's neck. "And the curse."

"How do you know about that?" Emma asked, clutching the pendant tightly.

Agnes smiled, though it wasn't a comforting smile. "I know many things, child. This curse has been in Hollowdale for centuries. You're not the first to be caught in its snare."

"Then you know how to break it?" Liam asked urgently.

Agnes nodded slowly. "Yes. The challenges you must face are part of the old magic—the magic that bound this town to the wolves long ago. The pendant is the key, but it also holds the curse within it."

"What are the other challenges?" Noah asked. "We've already faced the first one—the wolves."

Agnes's eyes narrowed. "The second challenge is one of heart. It will test your loyalty and your love for one another. The third challenge... well, you'll discover that soon enough."

"But how do we complete them?" Emma asked. "How do we know what to do?"

Agnes stood up and walked over to one of the shelves, pulling down a small, weathered book. She flipped through its pages and then handed it to Emma. The book was filled with strange symbols and illustrations, many of them depicting wolves, moons, and mystical rituals.

"That book will help guide you," Agnes said. "But be warned—the curse is not easy to break. You will have to make sacrifices, and the price for failure is high. If you do not complete the challenges before the next full moon, the curse will be permanent."

The weight of her words hung in the air, chilling the group.

"Permanent?" Mia whispered, her eyes wide.

"Yes," Agnes said, her voice grim. "You will become what the curse intends. A wolf. Forever bound to the night and the moon."

Emma swallowed hard. She could feel the pulse of the pendant against her chest, and for the first time, the reality of what was happening truly hit her. This wasn't just a game or an adventure. If they failed, her life would change forever.

Lessons from Chapter 5: The Old Witch's Warning

1. **Asking for help when you're unsure is a sign of strength, not weakness**: The group realized they couldn't solve the mystery on their own and sought out Agnes for guidance, showing that asking for help is a smart and brave decision.

2. **Old stories often hold valuable wisdom**: Agnes's knowledge of the curse and the pendant came from ancient legends. This teaches us that old stories and wisdom passed down can still be important today.

3. **Loyalty and love are powerful**: The second challenge will test the group's loyalty and love for each other, showing that these qualities are important when facing difficult challenges.

4. **Sacrifices are sometimes necessary to achieve goals**: Agnes warned that breaking the curse would require sacrifices. In life, achieving important goals often means making tough decisions and giving something up.

5. **Prepare for the unexpected**: The group now knows that breaking the curse will be more difficult than they thought. This teaches us that even when we think we're ready, life can throw unexpected challenges our way.

Chapter 6: The Enchanted Forest

After their visit to Agnes, the group realized how high the stakes were. Emma could feel the changes more acutely now. Her senses were sharper, and sometimes she caught herself glancing at the moon, feeling its pull even when it wasn't full.

They gathered once again at the edge of the woods, the place that seemed to hold all the answers. Emma clutched the weathered book that Agnes had given her, feeling the weight of its secrets. As they entered the woods, the trees seemed to lean in closer, as if the forest itself was alive and watching them.

"Is it just me," Mia whispered, "or does the forest feel... different?"

Liam, who was always the most level-headed, nodded. "It's like the woods know what we're doing. We need to be careful."

Noah shrugged, trying to appear casual even though his eyes darted nervously between the trees. "It's just a bunch of trees. Let's focus on finding the next challenge."

Emma opened the book, flipping through its worn pages until she found the passage Agnes had mentioned. There, written in a strange script, was a clue: *To break the second bond, the heart must lead where the mind cannot follow. In the forest, what is lost must be found again.*

"It's a riddle," Emma said, frowning. "But I think it means we need to find something. Something hidden in the forest."

"What could it be?" Noah asked, peering into the dense woods.

Liam took a deep breath. "Only one way to find out. Let's keep going."

They continued walking deeper into the forest, the trees growing thicker around them. The light filtered through the leaves, casting strange shadows on the ground. As they walked, the air grew heavier, and a thick mist began to roll in, making it hard to see more than a few feet ahead.

"This doesn't feel right," Mia said, her voice tight with worry. "What if we get lost?"

Emma glanced around. The forest did seem endless, and the mist made it feel even more disorienting. But something inside her—the pull of the pendant, perhaps—told her to keep going.

"We won't get lost," Emma said, trying to sound confident. "We'll know what we're looking for when we find it."

But as they walked, the mist thickened, and soon, they couldn't even see each other clearly. The trees around them seemed to shift and move, as if they were changing the path beneath their feet.

"I can barely see!" Noah shouted through the mist. "What's happening?"

"I think the forest is enchanted," Emma said, her voice shaky. "It's trying to confuse us."

Mia reached for Emma's hand, her grip tight. "We have to stay together."

Just then, the ground seemed to ripple beneath them, and Emma felt herself stumbling. She tried to keep her balance, but the mist swirled around her, pulling her away from her friends.

"Emma!" she heard Liam shout, but his voice was distant, fading into the mist.

Panic surged through her as she realized she was alone. The mist had swallowed her, separating her from the others. Her heart raced, and she could feel the pendant growing warmer against her skin, as if it was responding to the forest's magic.

"Stay calm," Emma whispered to herself. "Think."

She took a deep breath and tried to focus. The riddle had said they needed to find something lost in the forest. But what? She reached into her pocket and pulled out the pendant, holding it up to the faint light. The symbols glowed faintly, and she realized they were pointing in a specific direction.

"Follow your heart," she muttered. "That's what Agnes said."

With no other choice, Emma began walking in the direction the pendant pointed. The mist swirled around her, but she stayed focused, trusting the pendant to guide her.

After what felt like hours of walking, the mist suddenly cleared, revealing a small clearing in the woods. In the center of the clearing stood a large stone, covered in moss and ancient carvings. At the base of the stone was a small object, half-buried in the dirt.

Emma approached cautiously, her heart pounding in her chest. As she knelt down, she realized what the object was: a small, old locket, its surface worn with age.

"This must be it," Emma whispered, picking up the locket. The moment her fingers touched it, the pendant around her neck glowed brightly, and the carvings on the stone lit up with a soft, golden light.

Suddenly, the air around her changed. The mist cleared completely, and the path ahead became visible. Emma could hear the voices of her friends again, calling out for her.

"I found it!" she shouted, her voice breaking through the mist.

A moment later, the others appeared, stumbling through the last remnants of the fog. They looked disheveled but relieved to see her.

"Emma!" Mia cried, running up to her. "We thought we lost you!"

"I'm fine," Emma said, holding up the locket. "This is what we were looking for."

Liam examined the locket closely. "That must be the second part of the curse. It's connected to the heart somehow."

"I think it belonged to someone who was part of the curse," Emma said, her voice thoughtful. "Maybe a family member of the Silvers. The locket represents something lost, like the love or connection that was broken when the curse was cast."

Noah whistled. "That's pretty deep. But it makes sense."

Emma placed the locket in her pocket and looked around. The forest no longer felt threatening, and the mist had completely disappeared.

"We passed the second challenge," she said softly. "But there's still one more to go."

Lessons from Chapter 6: The Enchanted Forest

1. **Facing fears can help you grow stronger and braver**: The group braved the mysterious, enchanted forest, facing their fears to find what was lost, showing that courage leads to personal growth.

2. **Trust your instincts when you're uncertain**: Emma followed her instincts, guided by the pendant, even when she was separated from her friends. Trusting her intuition helped her navigate the forest and find the second clue.

3. **Sometimes you need to let your heart guide you**: The second challenge was about following the heart, not just logic. This teaches that sometimes, emotional intelligence is just as important as reasoning.

4. **Things are not always what they seem**: The enchanted forest tried to confuse and disorient them, but they realized that the magic was a test. This reminds us that not everything is as it appears at first glance.

5. **Stay focused when the path is unclear**: Even though the mist and forest were trying to lead them astray, the group stayed focused and determined. In life, when things are confusing, it's important to stay on course.

Chapter 7: The Path to the Hidden Lake

Emma kept the old locket tucked safely in her pocket, the cool metal occasionally brushing against her hand as they walked. She knew it wasn't just an ordinary locket—it was a symbol of the bond they had to restore, something connected to the heart.

Back in the clearing, they gathered around to rest. The tension from being separated in the mist had worn them out, and though they had passed the second challenge, none of them felt like celebrating.

"What do you think the third challenge will be?" Noah asked, his voice low. "The first one was about strength, and the second was about loyalty or love, right? What's left?"

Emma pulled out the weathered book from Agnes and flipped through the pages, hoping for some clue. Finally, she found a passage written in the same cryptic style as the others: *To break the third bond, you must journey where the water runs still, and the truth hides beneath. Only then will the full moon's curse be lifted.*

"Where the water runs still," Emma read aloud. "It must be talking about the lake."

Liam frowned. "The lake? You mean the one in the middle of the forest? That place is off-limits, even for camping."

"It makes sense," Mia said, nodding. "The lake is hidden, and there are a lot of legends about it. My parents told me stories about strange things happening there. If we're going to face the final challenge, that's probably where we'll find it."

Emma tucked the book away and stood up. "We don't have a choice. The full moon is getting closer, and if we don't break the curse before then..."

"We'll figure it out," Liam said, his voice full of confidence. "We've come this far. We can handle one more challenge."

The next morning, they set off early, following the old path that led deeper into the woods. The journey was long, and the path grew narrower as they ventured closer to the hidden lake. The trees became denser, their branches hanging low as if they were trying to keep people away. It felt as though the forest itself was guarding something.

After a few hours of walking, they arrived at the edge of the lake. The water was perfectly still, reflecting the gray sky above like a mirror. The air was eerily quiet, and not a single ripple disturbed the surface of the lake.

"There it is," Noah said softly, staring at the lake. "The hidden lake."

Mia shivered, wrapping her arms around herself. "I don't like this place. It feels... wrong."

Emma stepped closer to the water's edge, her eyes scanning the surface. There was something about the lake that made her uneasy, too. But she couldn't turn back now. The pendant around her neck pulsed faintly, as if urging her forward.

"There's something under the water," Emma said, her voice barely above a whisper. "I can feel it."

Liam glanced at her, concerned. "What do you mean? How can you feel something?"

Emma didn't have an answer. She only knew that the pendant, and the curse it carried, was guiding her. She knelt down by the water's edge, her reflection staring back at her in the stillness. Slowly, she reached out and dipped her hand into the water.

The moment her fingers touched the surface, the water rippled, and a strange, soft light began to glow from beneath the lake. The group stepped back, startled.

"What's happening?" Noah asked, his voice shaking.

"I think it's the third challenge," Emma said, standing up. "We have to find whatever's under the lake."

Liam looked uneasy. "You're not suggesting we swim, are you? This water's freezing, and we don't know how deep it is."

Emma nodded, though she could feel the nervousness building inside her. "We have to. It's the only way."

Without hesitation, Emma slipped off her shoes and waded into the water. The cold was sharp, biting at her skin, but she pushed forward, the light beneath the surface growing brighter as she moved deeper. The others followed, though Mia hesitated for a moment before stepping into the icy water.

As they swam farther from the shore, the light beneath them began to take shape. It was a large, glowing object, half-buried in the lakebed. Emma felt a strange sense of déjà vu, as though she had seen this place before—in her dreams, perhaps.

"Look!" Noah pointed. "There's something down there!"

Emma took a deep breath and dove beneath the surface. The cold water rushed over her, but she swam down toward the glowing object. As she got closer, she saw that it wasn't just a random object—it was a stone chest, covered in strange, ancient symbols. The same symbols she had seen on the pendant.

She reached out and touched the chest. The moment her fingers made contact, the chest unlocked, and the lid slowly slid open, revealing a small, intricate key made of silver. The key glowed brightly, illuminating the dark water around her.

Emma grabbed the key and swam back to the surface, gasping for air as she emerged. She held the key up for the others to see.

"I found it!" she called out, her voice echoing across the still lake.

The others swam to her, their eyes wide with amazement.

"What is it?" Mia asked, staring at the key.

"It's the key to the curse," Emma said, her heart pounding. "This is the final piece."

They swam back to shore, and as they reached the edge of the lake, the pendant around Emma's neck glowed even brighter. She held the key up to the pendant, and for a moment, the two objects seemed to resonate with each other, their lights merging into one.

Suddenly, a voice echoed through the forest, low and powerful: "You have found the key, but to break the curse, you must face the truth. Only then will the bond be broken."

The voice faded, and the forest fell silent once more.

Lessons from Chapter 7: The Path to the Hidden Lake

1. **Sometimes the most important answers are hidden beneath the surface**: The third challenge required the group to look beneath the surface of the lake, reminding us that the truth is often deeper than it seems.

2. **Perseverance leads to discovery**: Despite the cold and uncertainty, Emma and her friends didn't give up. Their determination helped them find the key to breaking the curse.

3. **Trusting the unknown can lead to growth**: The lake was mysterious and unsettling, but by trusting in the process and following the clues, the group learned valuable lessons about themselves and the curse.

4. **The journey isn't over until all parts are revealed**: Finding the key was only part of the challenge. The group learned that solving one part of a mystery often leads to deeper questions that must be faced.

5. **The truth is sometimes the hardest challenge**: The final test will require the group to face the truth about the curse and themselves. Facing the truth is often the hardest challenge, but it's necessary for growth and resolution.

Chapter 8: The Talking Trees

The key glowed faintly in Emma's hand as they made their way back through the forest, still wet and shivering from their swim in the hidden lake. The eerie silence of the woods pressed down on them, and though they had found the key, the group couldn't shake the feeling that the hardest part of their journey was yet to come.

As they walked, Emma kept turning the silver key over in her hand. It was intricately carved, with tiny symbols running along the edges—symbols that matched those on the pendant and the chest at the bottom of the lake. But the voice that had spoken when they found it still echoed in her mind: *"You must face the truth. Only then will the bond be broken."*

"What do you think that voice meant by facing the truth?" Mia asked, breaking the silence as they trudged along the narrow path. She was clearly uneasy, her gaze flitting nervously between the trees.

Liam sighed, rubbing the back of his neck. "I don't know. Maybe it means there's more to the curse than we realized. We found the key, but it sounds like there's one more challenge waiting for us."

"The hardest one," Noah muttered. "Great."

Emma looked around at the dense forest, noticing how the trees seemed to lean in closer, as if they were listening to their conversation. The wind rustled through the leaves, creating a low, whispering sound that made the hair on the back of her neck stand up.

"Do you hear that?" Emma asked, stopping in her tracks.

The group paused, listening. At first, it just sounded like the wind, but as the whispering grew louder, they realized it wasn't the wind at all. The trees around them were speaking—soft, hissing voices drifting through the branches.

"What is that?" Mia whispered, her eyes wide with fear.

Emma took a step closer to one of the trees, squinting at its rough bark. The whispers seemed to come from deep within the wood, a language they couldn't quite understand.

"I think... the trees are talking to us," Emma said softly.

Liam frowned. "Talking trees? Seriously?"

But as they stood there, the whispers became clearer. Slowly, the words started to take shape, and though the voices were soft and distant, Emma could finally make out what they were saying.

"Return the key... the truth lies within the heart of the forest... face the past, or the curse will remain..."

"Did you hear that?" Emma asked, turning to the others. "They said the truth lies in the heart of the forest."

Noah swallowed nervously. "So, what? We go deeper into the woods?"

Liam nodded, glancing down at the key. "Looks like it. If the trees are telling the truth, we have to go to the heart of the forest to face whatever this final challenge is."

Emma took a deep breath. "Then let's keep going."

They continued deeper into the woods, following the faint whispering of the trees as if it were a guide. The forest grew darker, the air colder, and the path more twisted with each step. But the pendant around Emma's neck kept glowing faintly, as if it were leading them forward, guiding them to the heart of the forest.

After what felt like hours of walking, they finally arrived at a clearing. In the center stood the oldest, largest tree they had ever seen. Its trunk was wide, gnarled, and ancient, with roots that twisted and curled out of the earth like the limbs of a giant. The tree's bark was covered in strange markings, similar to the ones on the pendant and key.

"This must be the heart of the forest," Emma said, stepping closer to the tree.

As she approached, the pendant grew warmer against her skin, and the whispers of the trees grew louder, surrounding them on all sides. The old tree seemed to hum with energy, and the air around it shimmered faintly with magic.

"Do we... do we talk to it?" Mia asked, her voice trembling.

Emma didn't answer. Instead, she reached out and placed her hand on the tree's rough bark. The moment she did, the pendant flared with light, and the tree seemed to come alive. Its branches swayed, and a deep, ancient voice rumbled from within its trunk.

"You have come," the tree said, its voice slow and resonant. "You seek the truth of the curse. But to break it, you must first understand it."

Emma's heart raced. "What do you mean? What is the truth?"

The tree's branches creaked as it spoke. "The curse was born from betrayal... from a broken bond of trust. The Silver family was once powerful, but their greed and jealousy turned them against each other. The pendant you wear was forged from that betrayal, and the curse has lingered ever since."

Liam stepped forward, his brow furrowed. "So, the curse was placed because of a family feud?"

"Yes," the tree replied. "But the curse is more than just a punishment. It is a reflection of the bond that was broken—between love, trust, and loyalty. To break it, you must restore that bond. Only then will the curse be lifted."

"But how do we restore it?" Emma asked.

The tree's branches swayed gently, and the key in Emma's hand began to glow. "The key you hold will unlock the final truth. But first, you must look within. You must face your own fears, your own doubts, and confront the truth about yourselves. Only then will the bond be restored."

The group exchanged uneasy glances. They had come so far, but now they realized that the final challenge wasn't just about finding the key or solving a riddle. It was about facing the deepest parts of themselves—the parts they had been avoiding.

Emma felt a lump form in her throat. "What if we can't do it?"

"You must," the tree said softly. "The truth is already within you. You only need the courage to face it."

The group sat down at the base of the old tree, the weight of the challenge pressing down on them. They had faced wolves, riddles, and an enchanted forest, but this challenge—facing the truth about themselves—felt more daunting than anything they had encountered.

Lessons from Chapter 8: The Talking Trees

1. **Listening to those with experience can provide wisdom and insight**: The ancient tree revealed the truth about the curse and the importance of understanding the past. Listening to wise voices can guide us when we're lost.

2. **The hardest challenges often come from within**: The group learned that facing the truth about themselves was the most difficult challenge. In life, our biggest obstacles can come from our own fears and doubts.

3. **Restoring broken bonds takes effort and understanding**: The curse was born from betrayal, and the only way to break it was to restore the bond of trust and love. This teaches that healing relationships takes time, effort, and understanding.

4. **Facing your fears is necessary for growth**: Emma and her friends were afraid of confronting their inner truths, but they realized that to grow, they had to face those fears head-on.

5. **Courage is found in facing the unknown**: The final challenge required the group to look deep within themselves, showing that courage comes from confronting the unknown, both in the world and in ourselves.

Chapter 9: The Wolf Inside

As night descended over the forest, the group huddled beneath the ancient tree, the glow of Emma's pendant casting faint shadows on their faces. The whispers of the trees had quieted, leaving the group alone with their thoughts. The key Emma held felt heavier now, as if the weight of the final challenge had doubled since they first found it at the hidden lake.

"We have to face our fears," Emma said, repeating the words of the old tree. "Whatever they are."

Liam nodded slowly. "But what if our fears are too big? What if we can't handle them?"

"We don't have a choice," Noah said, his voice firmer than it had been before. "We've come too far to turn back now. The full moon is almost here, and if we don't break the curse..."

Emma swallowed hard, finishing the thought in her head. *If we don't break the curse, I'll turn into a wolf under the next full moon. Permanently.*

The pendant around her neck pulsed faintly, as if responding to her thoughts. For a moment, Emma wondered if the transformation had already begun. She felt different—not just physically, but emotionally, too. Her senses were heightened, and she felt an unusual pull toward the forest, as though the wildness of the woods was calling to her. But at the same time, she was terrified of what that pull meant.

"I think the final challenge is more than just facing our fears," Emma said, looking at her friends. "It's about accepting them. If we're going to break the curse, we have to face the parts of ourselves we've been avoiding."

The group sat in silence for a moment, the truth of Emma's words sinking in.

"But how?" Mia asked softly. "How do we face something like that?"

"I don't know," Emma admitted. "But we have to try."

As they sat around the base of the tree, the forest around them began to shift. The air grew colder, and a faint mist rolled in, swirling around their feet like it had a life of its own. The tree's ancient branches creaked above them, and the whispers of the forest returned, soft and haunting.

Suddenly, the ground beneath them shuddered, and the earth split open at the base of the tree, revealing a deep, glowing fissure. From within the crack in the earth, shadows began to rise—dark, swirling figures that looked like living nightmares. They took on familiar shapes: wolves with glowing eyes, twisted figures from old legends, and ghostly forms that seemed to echo the deepest fears of each of them.

Mia gasped, stepping back. "What... what are those?"

"They're our fears," Emma whispered, her heart racing. She could feel her own fear rising within her, threatening to consume her. One of the shadowy wolves moved closer to her, its eyes gleaming like fire.

"Don't let them get to you!" Liam shouted, but even his voice shook with fear.

The shadows circled them, and Emma felt the pendant around her neck burn hotter. The shadows were feeding on their fear, growing stronger as the group's resolve weakened.

"I... I can't do this," Mia whimpered, her voice trembling. "I'm too scared."

"You can do it," Emma said, stepping toward her friend. "We all can. The tree said we have to face the truth—and the truth is, we're all afraid. But we have to accept that fear. It's part of us."

Mia looked at Emma, her eyes wide with fear. "But what if it's too much?"

Emma placed a hand on Mia's shoulder. "We're in this together. Just trust yourself."

As Mia took a deep breath and faced the swirling shadows, something changed. The wolf-shaped shadow that had been stalking her began to fade, its form losing shape as Mia stood her ground. The more she accepted her fear, the weaker the shadow became.

"It's working," Noah said, watching the shadows around them flicker and weaken. "We have to face our fears to beat them."

Each of them took a step forward, facing the shadowy figures that represented their fears. Emma felt her heart pounding as she stared at the wolf-shaped shadow that seemed to be a reflection of the curse inside her. The wolf's eyes gleamed, and its teeth bared in a snarl, but Emma didn't look away.

"I'm not afraid of you," Emma said, her voice steady despite the fear gnawing at her. "I know what you are—you're the curse. You're the part of me I've been afraid of. But I'm not running from you anymore."

The shadow wolf snarled, but as Emma stood her ground, it began to dissolve, its shape breaking apart like mist in the wind. She could feel the pull of the curse inside her, the part of her that had been changing since she put on the pendant, but she refused to let it control her.

As Emma faced her fear, the pendant around her neck glowed brighter, and the key in her hand began to vibrate softly. One by one, the shadows around them faded, their forms disintegrating as each of the friends confronted their own fears.

When the last shadow was gone, the ground beneath the ancient tree sealed itself once more, the glowing fissure disappearing. The forest was quiet again, the mist lifting to reveal the moonlight filtering through the trees.

Lessons from Chapter 9: The Wolf Inside

1. **Accepting your fears helps you overcome them**: Emma and her friends learned that the only way to break the curse was to face their deepest fears and accept them. In life, accepting your fears is the first step to conquering them.
2. **Your greatest battles are often internal**: The final challenge wasn't about fighting physical enemies—it was about

confronting the fears and doubts within themselves. Many of the hardest challenges we face are internal, not external.

3. **You are stronger than your fears**: By standing their ground and facing their fears head-on, the group discovered that they were stronger than the fears that had been holding them back.

4. **Facing fears together makes the journey easier**: The friends supported each other through the final challenge, showing that when we face difficult situations together, we become stronger and more capable.

5. **True growth comes from within**: The curse wasn't just about the pendant—it was a reflection of the inner battles the group had to fight. Personal growth happens when we confront and accept the parts of ourselves we fear the most.

Chapter 10: The Witch's Second Visit

The moonlight filtered softly through the trees as the group made their way back through the forest. The weight of the final challenge still hung over them, but a sense of relief filled the air. They had faced their deepest fears and broken the curse. At least, that's what they hoped.

As they walked, Emma kept glancing at the key in her hand. It no longer glowed, but it still felt important—like there was one last piece of the puzzle they hadn't uncovered yet. The pendant around her neck had grown warm again, a soft hum of energy flowing through it.

"We did it, right?" Mia asked, breaking the silence. "We broke the curse?"

Liam nodded, but he didn't look entirely convinced. "I think so. The shadows disappeared, and we faced our fears. That was the final challenge."

"But what if it wasn't?" Noah asked, his voice filled with uncertainty. "What if there's more we don't know?"

Emma glanced at the pendant again. "There might be. We faced our fears, but the curse was born from something deeper—betrayal, broken trust. What if there's still a piece of that curse left?"

They reached the edge of the forest and paused, the sight of Hollowdale's streets bringing a sense of comfort. But Emma couldn't shake the feeling that they weren't done yet. Something tugged at her—something unfinished.

"We need to talk to Agnes again," Emma said suddenly.

"Agnes?" Mia asked, her voice nervous. "But we've already seen her. She told us about the challenges, and we completed them."

"I know," Emma replied, her eyes fixed on the distant lights of Hollowdale. "But something doesn't feel right. I think she knows more than she told us."

Liam sighed but nodded. "Okay. Let's go."

The walk to Old Agnes's house felt longer this time, though it wasn't far. The group approached her crooked, weathered cottage with caution, the air around them heavy with uncertainty. The last time they had come here, Agnes had warned them that breaking the curse would require sacrifices. Emma wondered now what those sacrifices would truly be.

Liam knocked on the door, and once again, the door creaked open slowly. Agnes stood in the doorway, her sharp eyes gleaming in the darkness.

"I was wondering when you'd return," she said, her voice soft but knowing. "Come inside."

They followed her into the small, dimly lit room, the same dried herbs and strange symbols decorating the walls. Agnes sat down at the wooden table and motioned for them to join her. Emma took a deep breath and sat across from her, placing the key on the table.

"We faced the challenges," Emma began. "We broke the curse—or at least, we think we did. But something feels off. Is there more we need to do?"

Agnes smiled faintly, though it didn't reach her eyes. "You've done well, children. You've faced the trials, and you've unlocked the truth. But curses are tricky things. They're not easily broken."

Mia shifted uncomfortably in her seat. "So, we haven't broken it yet?"

Agnes leaned forward, her gaze intense. "The curse was never just about the pendant or the key. It was about what the pendant represents—the broken bonds, the betrayal of trust. The curse lives in the heart of those who hold onto the pain of the past."

"The Silver family," Liam said. "They placed the curse because of what happened between them."

Agnes nodded. "Yes. But the curse has lingered because that betrayal was never healed. The challenges you faced were designed to help you understand that. But to truly break the curse, you must go beyond that understanding."

Emma frowned. "What do you mean?"

Agnes reached out and touched the key lightly, her fingers tracing the symbols etched into the silver. "The final act of breaking the curse requires you to restore what was broken. The Silver family's curse was born from a broken trust between family members, and that trust must be restored."

"But the Silver family is gone," Noah said, confused. "How can we restore something if they aren't here?"

"The family is gone," Agnes agreed, "but the legacy of that betrayal remains. The pendant you wear, Emma—it's tied to that legacy. And you, all of you, are now tied to it, too."

Emma's heart raced. "So, we have to... what? Forgive them?"

"Forgiveness is part of it," Agnes said slowly. "But it's more than that. You must let go of the pain and the fear that the curse has carried with it. You must offer peace, not just for yourselves, but for those who suffered because of the curse."

The group was silent for a moment, absorbing her words. Mia spoke first, her voice soft but determined. "But how do we do that?"

Agnes stood and walked over to one of the shelves, pulling down an old, tattered scroll. She unrolled it carefully on the table, revealing an ancient map of Hollowdale, with strange symbols marking certain locations.

"There's one last place you need to go," Agnes said, pointing to a spot on the map deep in the woods. "The place where the curse was born. The old Silver family estate, now long abandoned."

Emma's eyes followed the path on the map, her stomach tightening. "What do we do when we get there?"

Agnes's gaze softened. "You'll know when the time comes. But remember, you've already done the hardest part. You've faced the truth, and you've unlocked the key to breaking the curse. Now, all that's left is to restore what was lost."

Lessons from Chapter 10: The Witch's Second Visit

1. **Sometimes, understanding the problem isn't enough—you must take action**: The group learned that understanding the curse and facing their fears was only part of the solution. To truly break the curse, they needed to take the final steps to heal what was broken.

2. **Forgiveness can help heal old wounds**: The curse was born from betrayal, and only through forgiveness and peace could it be broken. In life, holding onto anger and hurt can keep us trapped in the past.

3. **The final challenge may be the hardest**: Agnes warned the group that the last step would be difficult, reminding them that the greatest obstacles often come at the end of a journey.

4. **Healing requires letting go of pain**: The group realized that breaking the curse meant more than just completing challenges—it required letting go of the pain that had lingered for generations.

5. **You can be part of the solution, even if you weren't part of the problem**: The group didn't cause the curse, but they were the ones who had to break it. This teaches that sometimes, we are called to fix things that others have broken.

Chapter 11: The Town's Forgotten Past

The next morning, the group gathered at Emma's house, their expressions serious. They knew what lay ahead: the final step in breaking the curse. The map Agnes had given them marked the location of the old Silver family estate, but none of them had ever been there before. It was in the deepest part of the woods, hidden from view and buried under layers of time and mystery.

Emma stood at the kitchen table, tracing her finger over the map. "This is where we need to go," she said, pointing to the spot Agnes had marked. "It's the heart of the curse—the place where everything began."

"But if it's so important, why doesn't anyone in town talk about it?" Noah asked, leaning over the table to get a closer look. "You'd think people would remember something like a cursed family."

Liam shrugged. "Maybe they don't want to remember. The curse happened a long time ago. People forget, or they try to."

Mia nodded, but her expression was still uncertain. "I just don't understand why we're the ones who have to fix this. We're not connected to the Silver family, are we?"

Emma hesitated before answering. "Agnes said we're tied to the legacy of the curse because of the pendant. Maybe it's not about bloodlines—it's about the choices we make. We found the pendant, and now it's our responsibility to break the curse. Maybe that's how it works."

The room fell silent as they absorbed her words. Finally, Liam spoke. "Okay, so we know where we're going. But what exactly are we supposed to do when we get there? Agnes wasn't exactly clear about that part."

Emma sighed, brushing a strand of hair from her face. "She said we'd know when the time came. I guess we have to trust that."

Mia fidgeted with the sleeve of her jacket. "I still can't believe there's a whole estate out there, hidden in the woods. If the Silver family was so important, why did their story disappear?"

"I don't think it disappeared completely," Emma said thoughtfully. "It's just been forgotten. People in Hollowdale probably didn't want to remember what happened with the curse. They buried the past."

"But now it's coming back," Noah said grimly. "And we're the ones who have to deal with it."

The journey to the Silver estate took the better part of the day. The woods became denser the farther they went, the trees growing so tall and thick that the sunlight barely penetrated the canopy. The path they followed was overgrown and twisted, as if the forest itself was trying to keep people away from the place they were headed.

"Are we getting close?" Mia asked, her voice barely above a whisper.

Emma checked the map again. "We should be. It's just up ahead."

They continued walking, the air growing cooler and more still with each step. Finally, the trees parted, and they found themselves standing before what was left of the Silver estate.

It wasn't much to look at anymore. Time had not been kind to the once-grand estate. The remains of a large stone mansion stood at the center of the clearing, its walls crumbling and covered in moss. Broken windows stared out like hollow eyes, and the roof had long since caved in. Surrounding the mansion were the remnants of old gardens and courtyards, overgrown with wild vines and weeds.

"This is it," Emma said softly. "The place where it all began."

Noah whistled low. "This place is... creepy."

Liam took a deep breath. "So, what now?"

Emma stepped forward, her heart pounding in her chest. The pendant around her neck grew warmer as they approached the ruins, the soft hum of magic growing stronger. She could feel it pulling her toward the mansion, as if the pendant itself knew what needed to be done.

"We need to go inside," Emma said, walking toward the broken entrance of the mansion.

The others followed, their footsteps echoing in the stillness. Inside, the mansion was even more decrepit than it looked from the outside. The floors were rotting, and pieces of the ceiling had collapsed, leaving gaping holes above them. But despite its ruined state, there was something undeniably powerful about the place—an ancient energy that seemed to pulse in the air.

"It feels like the curse is still here," Mia whispered, glancing around nervously.

Emma nodded. "It is. This is where it all started, and this is where we have to end it."

They wandered through the main hall, their footsteps careful on the decaying floor. Emma's eyes were drawn to an old fireplace at the far end of the room. Above it, a large, cracked mirror hung on the wall. The moment she saw it, the pendant around her neck began to glow even brighter.

"This is it," Emma said, stepping closer to the mirror. "This is where the curse is tied."

Noah frowned, staring at the mirror. "What do we do with it?"

Emma reached out and touched the surface of the mirror. The glass felt cold beneath her fingers, and as soon as she made contact, the mirror began to ripple, as though it were made of liquid rather than glass.

Suddenly, the room around them seemed to shift. The crumbling walls flickered, and for a brief moment, they were no longer standing in a ruined mansion—they were in a grand, fully restored ballroom, filled with the sound of laughter and music. Figures danced around them, dressed in elegant clothes from centuries past, their faces blurred and indistinct.

"What's happening?" Mia gasped, staring at the scene around them.

Emma felt the weight of the pendant pull her closer to the mirror. "We're seeing the past. This is the Silver family, before the curse."

The figures continued to dance, but the atmosphere began to change. The laughter grew strained, the music dissonant. The dancers started to move faster, their faces twisting into expressions of anger and jealousy. The scene darkened, and Emma knew they were witnessing the moment the curse was born.

"We're seeing the betrayal," Emma whispered. "This is where it all went wrong."

The image in the mirror shifted again, and the scene dissolved into darkness. The ballroom faded, replaced by a single figure standing in front of the mirror—an old man, his face lined with anger and regret. He was holding the pendant, the same one that Emma now wore, and he muttered something under his breath, words laced with bitterness.

"I curse this family, and all who come after," the man said, his voice low and menacing. "Let them suffer as I have suffered."

The image in the mirror shattered, and the room around them returned to its ruined state.

Emma stepped back, her heart pounding. "That was the moment the curse was cast."

"But what do we do now?" Noah asked, his voice shaky.

Emma looked down at the pendant, feeling the weight of the key in her other hand. "We have to finish what he couldn't. We have to let go of the anger and the betrayal. That's the only way to break the curse."

Mia took a deep breath. "So, how do we do that?"

Emma didn't know the exact answer, but she could feel the truth deep inside her. They had to offer peace—peace to the Silver family, peace to the legacy of betrayal that had festered for so long. It wasn't just about breaking a curse; it was about healing a wound that had been left open for generations.

"We forgive them," Emma said quietly. "And we let go."

Lessons from Chapter 11: The Town's Forgotten Past

1. **Understanding history helps us learn from past mistakes**:
    The group learned about the Silver family's betrayal and how
    the curse began. Knowing the past helps us understand the
    present and make better decisions for the future.

2. **Forgiveness is key to breaking cycles of pain**: The curse was
    born from anger and betrayal, and only through forgiveness
    could it be broken. In life, holding onto grudges can keep us
    trapped in cycles of pain.

3. **The past is not always what it seems**: The group witnessed
    the moment the curse was cast, realizing that what they had
    heard about the past wasn't the whole truth. This teaches us
    to seek deeper truths before making judgments.

4. **Healing requires confronting the source of pain**: To break
    the curse, the group had to confront the source of the Silver
    family's suffering. Healing requires facing the root of the
    problem, not just the symptoms.

5. **Letting go is sometimes the hardest part**: Emma realized
    that to break the curse, they had to let go of the anger and
    betrayal that fueled it. In life, letting go of negative emotions
    can be one of the hardest but most necessary steps toward
    healing.

Chapter 12: The Graveyard at Midnight

The air felt heavy as the group stood in the remains of the Silver family's mansion, the echoes of the past still lingering in the shadows. The vision they had seen in the mirror—the betrayal, the anger, and the moment the curse was cast—had left them shaken. But now, they knew what needed to be done.

"We have to let go," Emma repeated, her voice steady despite the fear gnawing at her. "We saw how the curse was born—from betrayal and pain. The only way to end it is to offer peace."

Noah glanced around the crumbling room. "But how? It's not like we can just say we forgive them and call it a day."

"There's something more," Liam said, his eyes narrowing as he scanned the room. "We're missing one last piece."

Mia, who had been silent, spoke up softly. "The graveyard. Agnes mentioned something about it, remember? When we first talked to her, she said that the curse was connected to the family's final resting place."

Emma's heart skipped a beat. She had almost forgotten that detail. "Of course," she said, nodding. "The curse wasn't just about what happened in this mansion. It's tied to the whole family—and they're buried in the old graveyard."

The graveyard lay on the far edge of Hollowdale, a place most people avoided. It was old—older than the town itself, some said—and overgrown with vines and moss. The Silver family had been buried there long ago, their graves largely forgotten by the town's inhabitants. But if the curse was tied to their legacy, then that's where the final step would take place.

"We need to go to the graveyard," Emma said, her voice firm. "That's where we'll offer peace. That's where we'll end the curse."

By the time they reached the outskirts of the graveyard, the sky had darkened completely, and the full moon hung high above them, casting an eerie glow over the landscape. The iron gate leading into the graveyard was rusted and twisted, and the stone path leading through the graveyard was barely visible beneath the tangled undergrowth.

Mia shuddered, wrapping her arms around herself. "I hate graveyards. They always feel so... haunted."

"We're not alone here," Noah added, his eyes scanning the rows of gravestones that stretched out before them. The wind rustled through the trees, and the air was thick with tension.

Emma led the way, her heart pounding as they moved deeper into the graveyard. The pendant around her neck pulsed softly, guiding her toward the far corner, where the oldest graves lay. Her fingers tightened around the silver key she had retrieved from the hidden lake, knowing that it would play a part in the final act of breaking the curse.

As they reached the oldest part of the graveyard, the names on the gravestones became familiar. There, in a row, were the gravestones of the Silver family. Each stone was cracked and worn by time, but the names were still visible, etched deeply into the cold stone.

"This is it," Emma said quietly. "The Silver family's resting place."

The group stood in silence for a moment, staring at the graves. The wind seemed to die down, and the graveyard grew unnervingly still. It was as if the entire place was holding its breath, waiting for something to happen.

"So, what do we do now?" Liam asked, his voice low.

Emma stepped forward, kneeling in front of the largest gravestone—the one that bore the name of the man they had seen in the vision, the one who had cast the curse in his moment of anger. The pendant around her neck glowed brighter as she touched the gravestone.

"We let go of the past," Emma said softly. "We offer peace to the family—to the curse. It's the only way."

Taking a deep breath, Emma held the key up to the gravestone. As soon as the key touched the cold stone, the ground beneath them trembled, and the air around them shifted. A faint, glowing mist began to rise from the graves, swirling around them like a veil of light.

Noah took a step back, his eyes wide. "What's happening?"

"The curse," Mia whispered, her voice filled with awe. "It's breaking."

The glowing mist continued to rise, swirling around the Silver family's graves. Within the mist, faint figures began to appear—ghostly silhouettes of the Silver family, their faces soft and indistinct. They were no longer filled with the anger and betrayal that had fueled the curse for so long. Instead, they looked peaceful, as though they had been waiting for this moment of release.

Emma felt a wave of emotion wash over her. She had expected fear, but what she felt instead was a deep sense of sorrow and understanding. The curse had been born out of pain, and now, it was finally time to let that pain go.

"I forgive you," Emma whispered, her voice barely audible. "We all do."

Liam, Mia, and Noah stood beside her, their heads bowed in respect. Together, they offered the peace that the Silver family had been denied for so long. The glowing mist grew brighter, enveloping the gravestones, until finally, it began to fade, dissolving into the night sky.

As the last traces of the mist disappeared, the pendant around Emma's neck stopped glowing, and the silver key in her hand turned cold. The curse had been broken.

"It's over," Emma said softly, standing up. "We did it."

The group remained silent for a moment, letting the weight of what had just happened sink in. They had faced so much—challenges, fears, and the darkness of the curse—and now, it was finally over. The Silver family had been laid to rest, and the curse that had haunted Hollowdale for generations had been lifted.

"We should go," Liam said gently. "We've done what we came to do."

For the first time in a long time, the forest felt peaceful.

Lessons from Chapter 12: The Graveyard at Midnight

1. **Courage is needed to confront the past**: The group knew they had to visit the graveyard, despite its eerie atmosphere, to finish what they had started. In life, facing the past is often difficult, but necessary for closure.

2. **Offering peace can heal old wounds**: The curse was broken when Emma and her friends offered forgiveness and peace to the Silver family. Healing is often found through reconciliation and understanding.

3. **Some challenges require emotional strength, not just physical bravery**: Breaking the curse wasn't about fighting or solving riddles—it required the group to find the emotional strength to forgive and let go of the past.

4. **Letting go is an act of release**: The glowing mist and the spirits of the Silver family represented the curse being released. In life, letting go of anger and pain is often the most freeing act we can undertake.

5. **Every end is a new beginning**: The curse was broken, but the experience changed Emma and her friends forever. In life, every challenge we overcome marks the beginning of something new, shaping who we are moving forward.

Chapter 13: Emma's Sacrifice

The curse was broken. The Silver family had been laid to rest, and peace had returned to the graveyard and the forest beyond. As Emma and her friends made their way back to Hollowdale, a sense of relief washed over them. The heavy weight that had been pressing down on them for days finally lifted, and the cool night air felt lighter, calmer.

But as they approached the edge of the woods, Emma felt something she hadn't expected—a lingering pull from the pendant still around her neck. The glow that had once been warm and steady had dimmed, but it hadn't disappeared entirely. It flickered faintly, as if there was still something unresolved.

"We did it," Mia said with a soft smile, her voice filled with relief. "It's finally over."

Liam nodded, stretching his arms above his head. "Yeah. It's kind of hard to believe, but we actually broke the curse."

Noah chuckled, though the sound was strained. "I thought for sure we were going to end up as part of some creepy ghost story ourselves."

Emma smiled at her friends, but inside, she couldn't shake the feeling that something was still wrong. She touched the pendant lightly, feeling the faint pulse beneath her fingertips. The curse had been broken, yes—but the connection to the pendant hadn't been severed.

"Guys," Emma said quietly, stopping just before they reached the clearing that led back to Hollowdale. "I don't think it's over yet."

The others turned to look at her, their expressions puzzled.

"What do you mean?" Liam asked. "We broke the curse. We saw the Silver family's spirits leave. Everything is back to normal."

Emma shook her head, her voice steady but filled with uncertainty. "The pendant—it's still connected to me. I can feel it. The curse might be broken, but I'm still tied to this somehow."

Noah frowned. "But how? You're not a Silver. Why would you still be connected to the curse?"

"I don't know," Emma admitted. "But I think the pendant is more than just a symbol of the curse. It's... part of me now. Maybe breaking the curse wasn't enough to free me from it."

Mia's eyes widened with concern. "What are you saying? That you're still cursed?"

Emma hesitated. "I think there's one last thing I have to do."

The realization hit her with a sudden clarity. The pendant, the key, the trials—they had all been part of breaking the Silver family's curse. But the magic that had bound Emma to the pendant was still active. The connection hadn't been broken yet because Emma herself hadn't let go. She had to make a choice.

"I have to destroy the pendant," Emma said softly. "It's the only way to free myself from the last piece of the curse."

Liam stepped forward, concern etched on his face. "Are you sure? What if destroying it makes things worse?"

Emma met his gaze, her heart pounding. "I don't think it will. I think destroying the pendant will release the last bit of magic that's tying me to the curse. It's the only way I'll be free."

Mia clutched Emma's arm, her eyes wide with fear. "But Emma, what if something happens to you when you destroy it? You don't know what will happen."

"I don't," Emma admitted. "But I can't live with this connection. The curse might be broken, but I'll always feel tied to it if I keep the pendant. It's a part of me now, and I have to let it go."

The group fell silent, the weight of Emma's decision sinking in. They had come so far, broken the curse that had haunted Hollowdale for generations, and now Emma was about to make the ultimate sacrifice to sever her connection to the pendant.

"How do we destroy it?" Noah asked quietly.

Emma looked down at the pendant, the flickering glow barely visible now. She could feel the magic within it, the ancient power that had bound the Silver family to the curse. It was strong, but it was also fragile—like a thread that could be cut with the right action.

"We need to take it to the lake," Emma said. "The place where we found the key. The water there is connected to the magic. If I throw the pendant into the lake, the water will destroy it."

Liam nodded, though his expression was serious. "If that's what you want to do, we'll be with you."

The walk back to the hidden lake felt different this time. The forest no longer felt haunted or oppressive, but there was a quiet tension that hung over them. Emma led the way, the pendant around her neck growing colder as they approached the water.

When they reached the edge of the lake, the water was still and silent, reflecting the moonlight like a mirror. Emma stepped forward, the pendant in her hand now, its faint glow pulsing weakly.

"This is it," Emma said softly, turning to face her friends. "Once I throw it in, it'll be over."

Mia's eyes filled with tears, and she stepped forward, wrapping Emma in a tight hug. "Be careful, okay?"

Emma hugged her back, her heart swelling with gratitude for the friends who had stood by her through everything. "I will."

Liam and Noah stepped closer, both giving her a nod of encouragement. "We're here with you," Liam said quietly. "Whatever happens, we've got your back."

Emma turned back to the lake, the pendant feeling heavier in her hand now. She took a deep breath, her mind racing with thoughts of the journey they had been through—the trials, the challenges, the moments of fear and courage. And now, the final act.

Without another word, Emma tossed the pendant into the lake.

The moment the pendant hit the water, a soft light rippled through the surface. The glow spread out across the lake, illuminating the entire area with a warm, golden light. For a moment, it felt as though time itself had stopped, the air humming with energy.

Then, the light faded, and the water returned to its still, mirror-like state.

Emma stood at the water's edge, her heart racing. The pendant was gone, and with it, the last piece of the curse. She felt the weight lift from her shoulders, the connection to the magic finally severed.

"It's done," Emma said softly, turning to face her friends. "I'm free."

Lessons from Chapter 13: Emma's Sacrifice

1. **Selflessness is a powerful act of love**: Emma's decision to destroy the pendant was an act of selflessness. By letting go of the last connection to the curse, she ensured that no one else would be affected by it.

2. **Letting go can be difficult, but necessary**: Emma understood that holding onto the pendant would keep her tied to the curse. In life, letting go of something, even if it's hard, is often necessary for personal growth and freedom.

3. **Facing uncertainty requires courage**: Emma didn't know what would happen when she destroyed the pendant, but she faced the unknown with courage. Sometimes, the bravest thing we can do is step into the unknown.

4. **Friends provide strength during difficult times**: Emma's friends supported her throughout the entire journey, standing by her side when she made the hardest decision. In life, the support of loved ones can make all the difference.

5. **True freedom comes from within**: By destroying the pendant, Emma freed herself from the curse, but the true freedom came from her willingness to let go and move forward. Personal freedom often comes from the choices we make within ourselves.

Chapter 14: The Wolves Attack

The morning after Emma destroyed the pendant, a sense of peace hung over Hollowdale. The eerie tension that had gripped the town since the start of the full moon's cycle seemed to have vanished. The air felt lighter, and the shadows that had once seemed alive with menace were just that—shadows.

Emma woke up feeling relieved but also exhausted. She had barely slept after the events at the lake, her mind racing with everything they had been through. Her friends, too, were emotionally drained. They had gone to bed with the knowledge that the curse had been broken, and for the first time in days, they believed the danger was over.

But that peace didn't last.

It was Mia who noticed it first, early that afternoon. She and Emma were sitting outside Emma's house, enjoying the rare moment of calm, when Mia's eyes widened in fear.

"Emma," Mia whispered, her voice shaky. "Look."

Emma followed Mia's gaze toward the woods that bordered the edge of Hollowdale. At first, she saw nothing out of the ordinary—just trees swaying in the breeze. But then, as she looked closer, she noticed movement. Shadows were darting between the trees, quick and sleek, almost too fast to track.

Wolves.

"No," Emma breathed, standing up quickly. "It can't be."

Mia grabbed her arm, her voice trembling. "But we destroyed the pendant. We broke the curse. Why are they still here?"

The wolves moved in and out of the trees, their glowing eyes flickering in the shadows. There were more than just a few—there had to be at least a dozen, prowling at the edge of the forest, watching them.

Panic surged in Emma's chest. "We need to find the others."

Without another word, the girls ran through town, their hearts pounding as they raced to Liam's house. Noah was already there, and the moment they saw Emma and Mia, they knew something was wrong.

"What is it?" Liam asked, his face paling when he saw their expressions.

"It's the wolves," Emma said, her voice breathless. "They're back."

Noah frowned, his brow furrowing. "But the curse was broken. How could they still be here?"

Emma shook her head, trying to make sense of it. "I don't know. But they're at the edge of the woods, and there are more of them this time. It's like they're waiting for something."

Liam paced the room, his mind racing. "What if destroying the pendant wasn't enough? What if there's another part of the curse we didn't know about?"

"That's impossible," Mia said, her voice shaky. "We did everything Agnes told us to do. We faced the challenges, broke the curse, and destroyed the pendant. There shouldn't be anything left."

Emma's mind raced. She could still feel the strange pull of the pendant, even though it was gone. Something was unfinished, something they hadn't accounted for. But what?

"We need to get to the woods," Emma said firmly. "If the wolves are here, then the curse isn't fully gone. There's something we're missing."

The group approached the edge of the woods cautiously, the wolves still pacing in the shadows. Their glowing eyes followed the group's every movement, but they didn't attack. It was as though they were waiting for a signal, or perhaps something else.

Emma swallowed hard, her heart racing. She had thought they were done—that the wolves were tied to the curse, and once the curse was broken, they would be gone. But now she understood that the curse was more complicated than they had realized.

"They're waiting for something," Noah said quietly, his eyes scanning the treeline.

"I know," Emma replied, stepping closer to the edge of the forest. "But what?"

The wolves moved closer, their growls low and menacing. Emma could feel the tension rising, the air around them thick with anticipation. And then, from deep within the woods, a long, eerie howl echoed through the trees. The wolves immediately stiffened, their eyes locking onto Emma and her friends.

"Did you hear that?" Mia whispered, her voice trembling.

"It's coming from inside the forest," Liam said, his expression grim. "Something's leading them."

Emma's heart sank. Of course. She had thought the curse was tied to the pendant, but the wolves—the creatures of the forest—had been here long before the pendant had been forged. They weren't just a product of the curse; they were connected to the deeper magic of the land itself.

"We need to go in," Emma said, her voice steady despite the fear gnawing at her. "There's something in the forest, something that's still holding the curse. It didn't end with the pendant."

Liam glanced at the wolves, his jaw set with determination. "Are you sure? Those wolves look ready to tear us apart."

Emma nodded. "We have to. If we don't stop this now, the whole town could be in danger."

The group gathered their courage and stepped into the forest, the wolves circling them but keeping their distance. The air was thick with tension, every shadow seeming to hide some unseen threat. But Emma led the way, her senses heightened as they moved deeper into the woods, following the sound of the howling.

As they ventured deeper into the forest, the trees grew denser, and the air became cooler. The howling continued, growing louder and more urgent. It wasn't just a single wolf—it was a chorus, as though the very heart of the forest was calling to them.

Finally, they reached a clearing. In the center stood a tall, ancient tree, its branches twisted and gnarled. At the base of the tree was something that made Emma's heart stop: a stone altar, covered in moss and old, weathered runes. The altar pulsed with a faint, eerie light, and surrounding it were more wolves—silent, watching.

"This is it," Emma said softly. "This is the source."

Liam stepped forward cautiously. "But what do we do? How do we stop this?"

Emma stared at the altar, her mind racing. The pendant had been destroyed, but the power that had fueled the curse was still here—deep within the forest, tied to the ancient magic of the land. The pendant had been a part of it, but the real source of the curse was something far older, something that had existed long before the Silver family's feud.

"We need to sever the connection," Emma said, her voice firm. "The altar is feeding the wolves, giving them the power of the curse. If we destroy the altar, we destroy the last piece of the curse."

Mia's eyes widened. "How do we destroy something like that?"

Emma didn't know. But as she stepped closer to the altar, the faint glow grew brighter, pulsing in time with her heartbeat. She could feel the magic within it—ancient, powerful, and angry.

"We have to find a way," Emma said quietly. "We can't let the curse continue."

The wolves growled low, their eyes watching the group intently. The final battle with the curse was at hand, and this time, there was no turning back.

Lessons from Chapter 14: The Wolves Attack

1. **Things don't always go as planned**: Even though they thought the curse was broken, Emma and her friends realized that something was still unfinished. This teaches us that not all problems are solved easily or completely, and we must be prepared for unexpected challenges.

2. **Perseverance is key**: Despite thinking they were done, the group didn't give up when they saw the wolves return. They knew they had to keep fighting, showing that perseverance is crucial in overcoming obstacles.

3. **Courage comes from action**: Emma's decision to lead the group into the woods despite the wolves shows that real courage is about taking action, even when you're afraid.

4. **Sometimes, the problem is deeper than it seems**: The curse wasn't just tied to the pendant—it was connected to something far older. In life, some problems have deeper roots, and solving them requires getting to the core.

5. **Trust your instincts**: Emma's instincts led her to understand that the wolves and the altar were still part of the curse. Trusting your gut can often guide you to the right solution, even when you don't have all the answers.

Chapter 15: The Hidden Cave

The clearing around the ancient altar felt charged with energy, a low hum of magic that made Emma's skin prickle. The wolves, still circling the altar, watched the group intently. Emma could feel the weight of the situation pressing down on her—this was the true heart of the curse, the real source of the magic that had plagued Hollowdale for so long. And now, it was up to them to end it once and for all.

But how?

"We can't just walk up and destroy that altar," Noah said, his eyes flicking nervously between the wolves and the pulsing stone. "There's something powerful about it. If we break it the wrong way, who knows what could happen?"

Emma stepped closer to the altar, her eyes scanning the ancient runes carved into the stone. She felt drawn to it, not in the way the pendant had drawn her before, but in a deeper, more instinctual way. The magic here wasn't just old—it was ancient, primal, and deeply connected to the forest itself.

"There has to be a way," Emma said, her voice steady. "This altar is feeding the wolves, giving them their power. If we can stop that—if we can sever the connection—we'll end the curse."

Liam studied the altar with a frown. "But it's more than just the altar, isn't it? The pendant was part of the curse, but it wasn't the whole thing. This place, this magic—it's tied to the land, the forest. We need to find where it all started."

Emma's heart raced as Liam's words sank in. He was right. The altar was powerful, but it wasn't the origin of the curse—it was a conduit, a channel for something much older. The wolves, the magic, the pendant—it all led back to one place.

"The cave," Emma whispered, her eyes widening. "There's a cave deep in the forest. Agnes mentioned it once, when we first talked to her. She said it was the place where the magic was born."

Mia's eyes widened. "You mean there's more to this than just the altar?"

Emma nodded, her pulse quickening. "The cave is the real source. The altar is just a way to channel that power, to keep the curse alive. If we can find the cave and stop the magic at its root, we can end this for good."

Noah swallowed hard, glancing at the wolves, which were still watching them with glowing eyes. "So we have to go deeper into the forest. Great."

Liam took a deep breath. "It's our only chance. If we destroy the altar without breaking the curse at its source, we might make things worse. We need to find the cave."

The group set off into the woods, moving carefully through the dense trees. The wolves didn't follow, but Emma could feel their eyes on her, watching from the shadows. The forest grew darker as they ventured deeper, the trees twisting together to form a canopy that blocked out most of the light.

Every sound made Emma's heart race—the crunch of leaves underfoot, the rustling of branches in the wind. The further they went, the more oppressive the air became, as though the forest itself was trying to close in around them. But Emma pressed on, her instincts guiding her toward the cave.

After what felt like hours, they reached a rocky cliff face hidden behind a thicket of trees. The entrance to the cave was small, barely noticeable from a distance, but Emma knew instantly that this was the place they had been searching for. A faint glow emanated from deep within, the same eerie light that had pulsed from the altar.

"This is it," Emma said, her voice barely above a whisper. "The cave."

Mia hesitated at the entrance, her eyes wide with fear. "Are we sure about this? What if the magic inside is too powerful for us to stop?"

"We don't have a choice," Liam said, stepping forward. "If we don't stop it, the curse will keep going. We can't let that happen."

Noah nodded, though his face was pale. "Yeah. Let's just hope we don't end up cursed ourselves."

Emma led the way into the cave, the others following close behind. The air inside was cool and damp, and the walls were lined with strange, glowing symbols that seemed to pulse with life. The deeper they went, the brighter the light became, until finally, they reached the heart of the cave.

There, in the center of the chamber, was a pool of water—still and silent, yet glowing with an ethereal light. Surrounding the pool were more ancient symbols carved into the rock, each one pulsing faintly in time with the light from the water.

"This is the source," Emma said softly, staring at the glowing pool. "This is where the curse began."

Liam stepped forward, his eyes scanning the chamber. "What do we do now? How do we stop it?"

Emma's heart pounded as she stared at the pool. The magic here was strong, stronger than anything they had faced so far. She could feel it pulling at her, urging her to reach out, to touch the water. But she knew that if she did, the magic could consume her.

"We have to sever the connection," Emma said, her voice firm. "The altar is feeding the magic from this pool. If we disrupt the source, the magic will fade, and the curse will be broken."

"But how do we do that?" Noah asked, his voice tense. "We can't just throw something into the water, can we?"

Emma stared at the pool, her mind racing. She reached into her pocket and pulled out the key—the same key they had found at the hidden lake. The silver gleamed in the eerie light, and for the first time, Emma understood its true purpose.

"The key," she said softly. "It was never meant to be just for the pendant. It's the key to the magic itself."

Without hesitation, Emma stepped forward and knelt by the pool, holding the key above the glowing water. She could feel the magic thrumming beneath the surface, a living, breathing force that had been tied to the land for centuries. But now, it was time to end it.

Taking a deep breath, Emma plunged the key into the water.

The moment the key touched the surface, a blinding light exploded from the pool, filling the cave with a deafening roar. The ground shook beneath them, and the walls of the cave seemed to tremble as the magic surged and crackled through the air. Emma's heart pounded as she gripped the key tightly, holding it steady as the magic swirled around her.

Then, just as suddenly as it had started, the light faded. The pool of water grew still once more, its glow dimming until it was nothing but a faint shimmer in the darkness.

Emma stood up, her breath shaky but steady. "It's done," she whispered. "The connection is broken."

Lessons from Chapter 15: The Hidden Cave

1. **Exploration leads to discovery, even when the path is uncertain**: The group had to venture deeper into the unknown to find the true source of the curse. In life, sometimes we must push beyond our comfort zone to find the answers we need.

2. **Patience and persistence are key to solving complex problems**: The curse was far more complicated than they initially thought, but Emma and her friends didn't give up. In life, some problems require persistence and careful thought to solve.

3. **True solutions often lie beneath the surface**: The altar wasn't the real source of the curse—it was the cave and the ancient magic within. This teaches that sometimes, we need to look deeper to find the root of a problem.

4. **The right tools can help us overcome great challenges**: The key that Emma had carried throughout their journey turned

out to be the final piece in breaking the curse. In life, having the right tools—whether knowledge, skills, or support—can make all the difference.

5. **Bravery comes from knowing when to act**: Emma's decision to plunge the key into the pool showed true bravery. She understood that action was needed, even if it carried risks. In life, bravery often means taking decisive action when the moment calls for it.

Chapter 16: The Truth Revealed

The air inside the cave was still, the magic that had once pulsed through the chamber now gone. The pool of water, once glowing with an eerie light, was dark and silent. Emma stood by the edge, the silver key still in her hand, its purpose finally fulfilled. The curse that had bound the wolves, the Silver family, and the land itself had been broken, and yet, Emma felt a sense of unease settle over her.

"It's done," Liam said, his voice cutting through the silence. "We broke the connection."

Noah exhaled slowly, leaning against the cave wall. "I thought for sure something would go wrong. But... we actually did it."

Mia, who had been standing near the entrance, slowly stepped forward, her eyes wide as she looked at the now-silent pool. "So, it's over? The wolves, the curse... all of it?"

Emma nodded, though the weight in her chest hadn't fully lifted. "The magic is gone. The source of the curse was in this cave, and we severed it. The wolves won't be controlled by the magic anymore."

"But why do I still feel like something's not right?" Mia asked quietly.

Emma felt the same. There was a lingering tension, a sense that while the magic had been disrupted, the story wasn't fully over. She turned to Liam, who was still scanning the cave with a serious expression.

"There's something we're missing," Emma said softly. "The magic is gone, but we still don't know why this curse was placed in the first place. We've only seen pieces of the story—the Silver family, the betrayal—but we don't know the full truth."

Liam's brow furrowed. "You think there's more to it?"

Emma hesitated, then nodded. "The cave, the altar, the pendant—they're all connected, but I don't think we've seen the real reason why the curse was placed. We need to know the whole truth."

Mia shivered. "But if the magic is gone, how are we supposed to find out?"

Emma looked around the cave, her eyes falling on the strange, ancient runes carved into the walls. The runes had stopped glowing, but they were still there, etched deep into the stone. They were a language Emma didn't understand, but she knew they held the answers they were looking for.

"The runes," Emma said, stepping closer to the cave wall. "They're the key to understanding the curse. They were here long before the Silver family's feud, and they'll tell us the whole story."

Noah shook his head. "But we don't know how to read them."

Emma glanced down at the key in her hand. It had been more than just a physical object throughout their journey—it had been a guide, leading them through the challenges and trials. And now, she realized, it was also the key to unlocking the final truth.

"We don't need to read them," Emma said, holding the key up to the runes. "The key will show us."

The moment the key touched the runes, the cave lit up with a soft glow. The runes pulsed faintly, their symbols rearranging themselves into patterns and shapes that shifted and moved. The cave rumbled slightly, as if the very stones were waking from a long slumber.

Suddenly, the cave's walls seemed to melt away, and the group found themselves standing in the middle of a vision—a vision of the past.

They were in the same forest, but it looked different. The trees were taller, younger, and the air was filled with the sounds of laughter and life. In the distance, they could see the Silver family's mansion, grand and untarnished by time. The scene was peaceful—until it wasn't.

From the edge of the forest, a group of people appeared—members of the Silver family, dressed in fine clothes. They were arguing, their voices sharp and angry. The air around them crackled with tension, and though their words were too faint to make out, Emma knew that this was the moment the curse had begun.

The scene shifted again, this time showing the same man they had seen before—the patriarch of the Silver family—standing before the altar in the clearing, his face twisted with rage and betrayal. He held the pendant in his hand, his knuckles white from gripping it so tightly.

"I curse you," the man said, his voice echoing through the vision. "I curse this family, and I curse this land. Let all who come after suffer as I have suffered. Let them know the pain of betrayal and never find peace."

The man slammed the pendant down on the altar, and the ground beneath him trembled as the curse took root. The air grew cold, and the vision blurred as the magic spread, twisting the forest and its creatures, binding the wolves to the land and creating the curse that would haunt Hollowdale for generations.

The vision faded, and Emma and her friends were once again standing in the cave, the soft glow of the runes dimming.

"That's it," Liam said, his voice filled with awe. "That's how it all started."

"The curse was born from betrayal," Mia whispered. "It wasn't just about magic. It was about the pain of what happened between the Silver family."

Emma stood in silence, the weight of the revelation sinking in. The curse had been more than just a spell—it had been born out of the raw, human emotions of anger, pain, and betrayal. The magic had been tied to those emotions, feeding off them for centuries.

But now, the connection had been severed. The curse was gone, but the legacy of that pain remained.

"What now?" Noah asked softly. "The curse is broken, but does that mean everything is okay?"

Emma looked around at her friends, her heart heavy but clear. "We've broken the magic, but the truth is that the curse was never just about the wolves or the pendant. It was about the family's pain. And now that we know the truth, we have to make sure that the past doesn't repeat itself."

Liam nodded. "We have to protect the town. Make sure the magic never comes back."

Mia sighed softly. "But how do we do that? How do we keep something like this from happening again?"

Emma smiled faintly, the weight of her journey lifting slightly. "By remembering the truth. By remembering what happened and making sure we don't fall into the same traps—of anger, of betrayal. The curse only had power because of the pain behind it. We have to make sure that kind of pain doesn't take root again."

Lessons from Chapter 16: The Truth Revealed

1. **The truth is often hidden, and it takes effort to uncover it**: The group had to delve deep into the history of the curse to understand its true origin. In life, finding the truth often requires digging beneath the surface.

2. **Pain and betrayal can create lasting consequences**: The curse was born from the Silver family's betrayal, showing that unresolved pain and anger can have lasting effects on future generations. Healing from betrayal requires addressing the root cause.

3. **History teaches valuable lessons**: By uncovering the truth about the Silver family, Emma and her friends learned the importance of understanding the past. In life, knowing our history helps us avoid repeating mistakes.

4. **Emotions can be as powerful as magic**: The curse wasn't just about spells or rituals—it was tied to deep emotions like anger and betrayal. This teaches us that emotions, if left unchecked, can have powerful and destructive consequences.

5. **Healing begins with knowledge**: Breaking the curse wasn't

just about ending the magic—it was about understanding the pain that had caused it. In life, healing often begins with understanding the source of the hurt.

Chapter 17: The Sorcerer Among Us

As Emma and her friends made their way back to Hollowdale, the weight of the truth they had uncovered hung over them like a storm cloud. The magic that had fueled the curse was gone, but there was an unsettling feeling in the air—like they hadn't yet faced the final danger. Though the wolves no longer prowled the woods, something deeper, something darker, still lingered.

The sun was setting by the time they reached the town, casting long shadows across the streets. The once-familiar town of Hollowdale now seemed different. More ominous. The group exchanged uneasy glances, feeling as though they were being watched.

"There's something wrong," Emma said, her voice low. "The curse is broken, but it feels like something else is still out there."

Liam nodded, his expression grim. "We've been chasing the source of the curse, but what if someone—or something—was controlling the magic this whole time? There's been too much power behind it for it to just be the curse alone."

"Wait," Mia said, her eyes widening in realization. "Do you think someone in the town knew about the curse all along? That maybe someone's been feeding the magic?"

The group fell silent as the thought took root. It was unsettling to think that someone in Hollowdale might have been manipulating the curse from the shadows, fueling it for their own purposes. But as much as they didn't want to believe it, the possibility was there.

Noah spoke up, his voice filled with concern. "So, if someone was controlling the curse, that means... they're still here. And they're still dangerous."

Emma clenched her fists, determination building inside her. "If that's true, we need to find out who it is. We can't let anyone keep playing with this kind of magic."

The group made their way to Agnes's house. If anyone knew who could be behind the lingering magic, it was the old woman who had guided them through the curse from the beginning. When they arrived, Agnes was waiting for them at her door, as though she had sensed their approach.

"You've uncovered the truth, haven't you?" Agnes asked, her voice quiet and knowing.

Emma nodded. "We know how the curse started, and we broke the connection in the cave. But something still feels wrong. We think someone has been controlling the magic all along."

Agnes's eyes narrowed. "You're more perceptive than I thought, child. You're right—there is someone who has been keeping the magic alive. But breaking the curse only weakened their power. The real threat remains."

"Who is it?" Liam asked, stepping forward. "Who's behind all of this?"

Agnes hesitated for a moment, then sighed deeply. "It's not someone from the Silver family, as you might have thought. The true source of the lingering magic lies with someone else—someone who has lived among you, hidden in plain sight."

Emma's heart raced. "Who?"

Agnes stepped back and motioned for them to enter her small, dimly lit home. The air inside was thick with the scent of herbs, and strange symbols lined the walls, much like the ones they had seen in the cave. As the group sat down around the table, Agnes pulled out an old, tattered book—one that looked even older than the book she had given them before.

"This," Agnes said, placing the book on the table, "is the history of Hollowdale. Most people think this town's story began with the Silver family and their curse, but Hollowdale's magic runs much deeper than that."

She opened the book to a page filled with old drawings and handwritten notes, pointing to an image of a man dressed in long robes, surrounded by symbols of power.

"This," Agnes said, "is the true source of the magic that has plagued your town. Long before the Silver family lived here, there was a sorcerer who practiced dark magic in these woods. He was feared by the people, but his power grew stronger every year."

Noah leaned in, his eyes wide. "So the curse didn't start with the Silver family?"

"No," Agnes said, shaking her head. "The curse was merely a byproduct of the sorcerer's magic. When the Silver family feuded, their anger and betrayal allowed the sorcerer's magic to take root in the land. The pendant you destroyed? That was created with his power."

Emma's stomach turned. "So, the magic we've been fighting this whole time—it wasn't just about the curse. It was about the sorcerer's influence."

"Yes," Agnes confirmed. "And that influence has remained in Hollowdale for centuries. The sorcerer's magic didn't die with him. He found a way to bind it to the land, and over time, someone in the town took control of that power. Someone has been manipulating the curse to keep the magic alive."

"But who?" Mia asked, her voice barely a whisper.

Agnes closed the book and met Emma's gaze. "The sorcerer's magic has passed down through generations. Someone in Hollowdale has inherited his power—and I believe that person is someone you know well."

The room fell silent as the gravity of Agnes's words sank in. Emma's mind raced, trying to think of anyone in town who could possibly have such power. Someone they had trusted? Someone who had seemed like part of their normal lives?

"Who?" Emma asked again, her voice barely above a whisper.

Agnes hesitated for a long moment, then spoke the name they had least expected.

"The mayor."

Shock rippled through the group. The mayor? The same man who had overseen every festival, every town meeting, every moment of their lives? He had always seemed so ordinary, so... harmless.

"No," Liam said, shaking his head. "That can't be right."

"It is," Agnes said firmly. "The mayor's family has controlled the magic for generations. His ancestors were sorcerers, and he has inherited their power. For years, he has kept the curse alive, using the town's belief in the Silver family's legacy to hide his true intentions."

"But why?" Emma asked, her voice filled with disbelief. "Why would he want to keep the curse going?"

Agnes's face darkened. "Power. The curse gave him control over the town, over the wolves, over the land itself. By keeping the magic alive, he was able to manipulate the people of Hollowdale without anyone suspecting him. But now that you've broken the connection, his power is weakening. He'll be desperate to regain control."

Noah's fists clenched. "So what do we do? We can't let him keep using the magic like this."

Agnes stood, her eyes hard. "You must confront him. But be careful—he still has power left, and he will do anything to keep it."

Emma's heart pounded. The truth had finally been revealed, and now, they knew their final enemy. The sorcerer's magic hadn't died with the curse—it had lived on in the mayor, hidden in plain sight. And now, it was up to them to stop him before he could regain control.

"We'll stop him," Emma said, her voice steady with determination. "We'll end this, once and for all."

Lessons from Chapter 17: The Sorcerer Among Us

1. **Trusting your instincts can help you find the truth**: Emma's feeling that something was still wrong led them to uncover

the truth about the sorcerer's magic. Trusting your instincts can often guide you to uncover hidden truths.

2. **The truth may be closer than you think**: The mayor, someone who had lived among them for years, was behind the lingering magic. This teaches us that sometimes, the most dangerous threats come from those we least expect.

3. **Power can corrupt over time**: The mayor had used the curse and the sorcerer's magic to gain power over Hollowdale. In life, unchecked power can lead to dangerous consequences.

4. **History can shape the present**: The group learned that the curse was part of a much larger story that dated back long before the Silver family. In life, the events of the past often influence the present more than we realize.

5. **Facing the truth requires courage**: Emma and her friends had to confront the difficult truth about someone they had trusted. In life, facing hard truths can be painful, but it is necessary for growth and justice.

Chapter 18: The Mayor's Secret

The idea that the mayor—someone they had all trusted—had been secretly controlling the curse for years was almost too much to process. But there was no time to dwell on it. If Agnes was right, the mayor would know his power was weakening, and he would do whatever it took to regain control.

"We need a plan," Liam said as they walked through the quiet streets of Hollowdale, their faces lit only by the fading glow of the evening sky.

Emma nodded, her mind racing. "We can't just confront him outright. He's still dangerous, and if he has any of that magic left…"

"He could use it against us," Noah finished, his face grim. "And who knows how many people in town are on his side? He's been the mayor for years—people trust him."

Mia shivered, pulling her jacket tighter around her shoulders. "But we have to stop him. If he's been controlling the magic, keeping the curse alive, who knows what else he's capable of?"

Emma knew Mia was right. They had already faced so much—wolves, haunted woods, ancient curses—and now it felt like everything had led to this moment. But confronting the mayor wasn't just about stopping a man who had hidden his power for years; it was about protecting Hollowdale from falling under his control again.

"We'll go to the town hall," Emma said after a moment of silence. "That's where he'll be. We need to expose him before he can figure out a way to use his magic against us."

"Expose him?" Liam asked, raising an eyebrow. "How do we do that without proof?"

Emma held up the silver key, the one that had led them through the challenges and revealed the truth in the cave. "This. The mayor's power is tied to the same magic that was in the cave. If we can use this to disrupt his connection to the magic, it'll weaken him enough for us to stop him."

"But what if it doesn't work?" Noah asked, his voice tense. "What if he's stronger than we think?"

Emma looked at her friends, her heart pounding. "Then we'll have to rely on our own strength. We've faced worse before. We can do this."

The town hall loomed in front of them, its tall windows dark as the last light of the day faded. The streets were quiet, but a strange tension hung in the air, as if the town itself was holding its breath, waiting for something to happen.

As they approached the front doors, Emma's heart raced. Her hand tightened around the key, its weight feeling heavier than ever. She knew what was at stake, and though fear gnawed at her, she pushed it down, focusing on what they had to do.

"We'll split up," Emma said, turning to the others. "Noah, Mia, you check the mayor's office. See if you can find anything that proves he's been controlling the magic. Liam and I will confront him."

Noah nodded, his face pale but determined. "We've got this."

Mia swallowed hard but nodded as well. "Be careful, okay?"

Emma gave her a reassuring smile. "We will."

As Noah and Mia slipped into the shadows, making their way toward the mayor's office, Emma and Liam headed toward the main hall. The large double doors creaked as they pushed them open, revealing the vast, empty room where town meetings were usually held. The echo of their footsteps filled the space, and for a moment, everything was still.

Then they saw him.

The mayor stood at the far end of the hall, his back to them as he stared out one of the tall windows. He didn't move as they approached, but Emma could feel the tension in the air, the unmistakable sensation of magic swirling around him.

"You've come," the mayor said without turning around, his voice calm but laced with something darker. "I was wondering when you'd figure it out."

Emma's heart pounded. "We know what you've been doing," she said, her voice steady. "The curse, the magic—it's been you all along."

The mayor finally turned, his face illuminated by the last rays of the setting sun. He looked older, more worn than Emma had ever noticed before, but there was something else in his eyes—a coldness, a hunger for power that sent a chill down her spine.

"You're right," the mayor said slowly, his lips curling into a small, humorless smile. "I've been keeping the magic alive. For generations, my family has controlled the power of the land, and I've done what I had to do to maintain that control."

Emma took a step forward, her grip tightening on the key. "But the curse was broken. We destroyed the pendant, severed the magic in the cave. It's over."

The mayor's eyes narrowed, his smile fading. "You think you've won? You think breaking a few connections is enough to stop the magic? You don't understand what you're dealing with."

Liam stepped beside Emma, his fists clenched. "Then why don't you explain it to us? Tell us why you've been using magic to control the town."

The mayor's gaze flicked to Liam, and for a moment, his expression softened. "You're young. You don't understand the burden of power. My family was entrusted with this magic centuries ago. It's not about control—it's about keeping balance, protecting the town from forces you can't begin to comprehend."

"By keeping them trapped in fear?" Emma shot back, her voice rising. "By using wolves and curses to control people?"

The mayor's face hardened. "Fear is a tool. One that keeps the peace."

Emma shook her head. "No. Fear isn't peace. You're not protecting anyone. You're only protecting yourself and your power."

For a moment, the room fell silent. The mayor's eyes darkened, and Emma felt the magic in the air grow stronger, crackling with energy.

"Enough," the mayor said, his voice sharp. "I won't let you take this from me."

He raised his hand, and a wave of energy surged through the room. Emma barely had time to react before the force of the magic hit her, knocking her back. Liam rushed forward, but the mayor flicked his wrist, sending him crashing into the far wall.

"Emma!" Liam called out, struggling to stand.

Emma scrambled to her feet, the key still clutched in her hand. The mayor's magic was strong—stronger than she had anticipated—but she wasn't going to back down now.

"You're right," Emma said, her voice steady. "I don't understand everything about magic. But I know this."

She raised the key, its silver surface gleaming in the dim light.

"The magic in this town doesn't belong to you anymore."

The mayor's eyes widened as Emma thrust the key forward, the air around her shimmering with the faint glow of the magic she had learned to control.

The room exploded with light.

Lessons from Chapter 18: The Mayor's Secret

1. **Power, if unchecked, can corrupt even the most trusted people**: The mayor, once trusted by the town, had allowed his family's magic to corrupt him, showing that unchecked power can lead to dangerous consequences.

2. **Courage is standing up to those in authority when they're wrong**: Emma and her friends showed bravery by confronting someone in a position of power, knowing it was the right thing to do, even if it was dangerous.

3. **Fear is not the same as peace**: The mayor used fear to control the town, but Emma understood that real peace cannot be built on fear. True peace comes from trust and understanding.

4. **Knowledge is a powerful weapon**: Emma and her friends learned that understanding the history of the magic and how it worked gave them the strength to stand up against the mayor. In life, knowledge is one of the most powerful tools we have.

5. **Confronting evil requires unity**: Emma, Liam, and the rest of the group stood together against the mayor's magic, showing that when people unite against a common threat, they are stronger together.

Chapter 19: The Battle of Magic

The blinding light filled the entire town hall, crackling with power as Emma thrust the silver key toward the mayor. The air shimmered with the raw force of magic, and for a moment, Emma felt the two opposing forces—her magic and the mayor's—clashing in the space between them.

The mayor's eyes widened in shock, and he stumbled backward, his grip on the magic faltering. He hadn't expected Emma to have this kind of power, but now it was clear that she had become more than just a girl trying to break a curse. She was a force in her own right.

"Emma!" Liam shouted, scrambling to his feet as the shockwave from the blast knocked over chairs and sent papers flying through the room. "Are you okay?"

Emma's whole body trembled with the force of the magic flowing through her. It wasn't the same as the dark magic the mayor wielded—it was something purer, something connected to the land and the ancient forces she had tapped into during their journey. She could feel the energy of the cave, the wolves, and the forest all surging through her, guiding her.

"I'm fine," Emma said through gritted teeth, though the weight of the magic pressed down on her like a heavy blanket. "We can't let him regain control."

The mayor stood at the far end of the hall, his face twisted in fury. His hands crackled with dark energy as he raised them, sending a wave of shadowy magic hurtling toward Emma and Liam.

Emma barely had time to react before the wave of magic hit, but this time, she was ready. She raised the silver key, and a shield of light appeared in front of her, blocking the mayor's attack. The shadows dissipated as they hit the barrier, leaving the air crackling with tension.

"You don't understand," the mayor snarled, his voice filled with desperation. "This power isn't something you can control! It's older than all of us—older than the town itself! You think you've won by breaking the curse, but you're only delaying the inevitable!"

Liam stepped forward, his fists clenched. "We broke your hold on the magic, and we'll break your control over the town, too."

The mayor's eyes flashed with anger, and another surge of dark energy filled the room. This time, it was stronger, more intense, and Emma could feel the weight of it pressing down on her. She knew she couldn't hold him off much longer—his power, though weakened, was still formidable.

But she wasn't alone.

Just as the mayor's magic bore down on them, a burst of light appeared from the side of the room. Noah and Mia had returned, and Noah was holding something in his hands—an old book, one of the ancient texts they had found in the mayor's office.

"We found it!" Noah shouted, running toward Emma and Liam. "This is how he's been controlling the magic!"

The mayor's face went pale as he saw the book in Noah's hands. "No!" he bellowed, his voice shaking with fury. "You don't know what you're dealing with! Put that book down!"

Mia grabbed Noah's arm and tugged him back as the mayor's dark magic lashed out again, but this time, the group was ready. Emma raised the silver key, channeling the pure magic of the land, while Noah opened the book and began reading from its pages. The ancient symbols on the pages glowed faintly, and the air around them seemed to hum with power.

"This is it!" Noah called out. "These are the binding spells he's been using to control the magic!"

Emma felt the silver key pulse in her hand, and as Noah read the spells aloud, she could feel the mayor's magic weakening. The dark energy in the room began to fade, the shadows receding as the ancient binding spells took hold. The mayor's grip on the magic was slipping, and Emma knew they were close to defeating him.

The mayor's face twisted in rage, and he lashed out with a final, desperate blast of magic. The force of it sent a shockwave through the room, shattering windows and knocking over chairs. Emma staggered backward, the silver key glowing brightly in her hand as she struggled to keep the shield of light in place.

"You don't understand!" the mayor shouted, his voice hoarse with desperation. "If you take this magic from me, you'll doom the town! Hollowdale needs this power to survive!"

"No!" Emma shouted back, her voice filled with conviction. "Hollowdale doesn't need your magic! The people of this town can live without fear and darkness—they deserve to be free!"

The mayor's magic flickered, and for a moment, Emma saw the truth in his eyes. Beneath the fury and desperation was fear—fear of losing the power that had defined him for so long, fear of being forgotten. He had clung to the magic for so many years, convinced that it was the only way to protect the town, but in doing so, he had become its greatest threat.

"It's over," Emma said softly, her voice carrying across the room. "Let it go."

The mayor's hands trembled, the dark magic faltering in the air around him. He looked at Emma, his eyes filled with bitterness, but also with resignation. For a long moment, the room was silent, the tension hanging in the air like a thread waiting to snap.

Then, with a final, pained cry, the mayor dropped to his knees, the dark energy around him dissipating into nothingness. The magic was gone, and with it, his hold over Hollowdale.

Emma lowered the silver key, her body trembling with exhaustion. The battle was over.

Liam rushed to her side, catching her as she staggered. "Emma, are you okay?"

"I'm fine," Emma whispered, though her whole body felt drained. "It's over."

Noah and Mia ran over, their faces filled with relief. "You did it," Noah said, his voice breathless. "We stopped him."

The mayor lay on the floor, defeated, the dark magic that had once made him so powerful now gone. He looked up at Emma, his eyes filled with a mixture of hatred and sorrow.

"You think you've won," he said, his voice barely a whisper. "But you've only just begun to understand the power of this land. The magic will return... someday."

Emma met his gaze, her expression calm. "Maybe. But when it does, we'll be ready."

Lessons from Chapter 19: The Battle of Magic

1. **True power comes from understanding, not control**: The mayor sought to control the magic for his own purposes, but Emma and her friends realized that true power comes from understanding and respecting the forces around them.
2. **Working together is the key to success**: Emma, Liam, Noah, and Mia worked as a team to confront the mayor and weaken his hold over the town. In life, teamwork and collaboration are often the key to overcoming difficult challenges.
3. **Letting go of power is difficult but necessary**: The mayor's desperation to hold onto his magic showed that letting go of power can be one of the hardest things to do, but it's often necessary for growth and healing.
4. **Standing up for what's right takes courage**: Emma's decision to confront the mayor, despite his power, was an act of great bravery. Doing what's right often requires facing difficult and dangerous situations.
5. **The end of one battle is the beginning of another journey**: Although they defeated the mayor, Emma knows that the magic of the land may return one day. Life is a series of challenges, and overcoming one doesn't mean the journey is

over—it means you're ready for the next step.

Chapter 20: A New Beginning

The dust settled in the town hall as the mayor's magic faded away, leaving behind only silence. Emma, Liam, Noah, and Mia stood over him, still catching their breath after the intensity of the battle. The mayor remained on the ground, his eyes dull and empty now that the dark magic had been stripped from him. The power that had fueled him for so long was gone, and with it, his influence over Hollowdale.

It was over.

For a moment, none of them spoke. The weight of what had just happened was too heavy for words. They had defeated the mayor, broken the curse, and saved Hollowdale from the ancient magic that had controlled it for centuries. But in the aftermath, there was only exhaustion and a quiet sense of disbelief.

"We did it," Noah said finally, his voice barely above a whisper. "It's really over."

Mia nodded, her hands still trembling. "I can't believe it. After everything... it's done."

Emma stood in silence, staring at the mayor as he lay on the ground. His power had been stripped away, and though he had once been the most powerful person in Hollowdale, he was now just an ordinary man. There was no more magic, no more darkness—just a broken man who had lost his way.

"What do we do with him now?" Liam asked, his voice steady but filled with unease. "He's not a threat anymore, but we can't just leave him here."

Emma glanced at the others, her heart heavy. She knew that the mayor needed to answer for what he had done, but there was no satisfaction in his defeat. He had been consumed by the magic, blinded by his desire for control, and now that it was gone, all that was left was the wreckage of his choices.

"We'll take him to the authorities," Emma said quietly. "He needs to be held accountable for what he's done, but... it's not our place to punish him. We've done what we needed to do."

Liam nodded, understanding. "You're right. He'll face justice, but we can't be the ones to decide that."

As they helped the mayor to his feet, his once fierce expression had softened into one of weariness and defeat. His eyes flicked between them, but there was no fight left in him. For the first time, he looked vulnerable, even lost.

"You think you've saved Hollowdale," the mayor said, his voice weak. "But there are forces in this world you don't understand. The magic of this land... it won't disappear just because you broke a few spells. You can't protect the town forever."

Emma met his gaze, her expression calm but firm. "We're not trying to protect Hollowdale from magic. We're trying to protect it from people who would use magic for the wrong reasons. The magic isn't evil, but it can be dangerous in the wrong hands. We'll make sure it's not misused again."

The mayor said nothing, his shoulders slumping in resignation. They led him out of the town hall and handed him over to the authorities, who had been alerted by the strange occurrences during the battle. As the mayor was taken away, the townspeople began to gather, whispering to each other about what had happened. The truth about the curse and the magic was spreading, and for the first time in years, Hollowdale was free from its shadow.

That evening, the group gathered at Emma's house, sitting quietly in the living room as the events of the day finally caught up with them. The atmosphere was a mixture of relief and exhaustion, but there was also a sense of closure. They had done it—they had saved their town.

"It feels strange," Mia said softly, her voice breaking the silence. "We've spent so long fighting the curse, and now that it's over... I don't know what to do next."

Liam leaned back in his chair, his arms crossed over his chest. "I know what you mean. We've been so focused on breaking the curse that it's hard to imagine life going back to normal."

Noah smiled faintly. "What even is normal after something like this?"

Emma chuckled, though her laughter was tinged with exhaustion. "I don't know. But whatever it is, it's going to feel weird for a while."

They all laughed, the tension in the room lifting just a little. The weight of the past few days had been overwhelming, but now that it was over, they could finally breathe again. The curse was broken, the magic had been tamed, and for the first time in a long time, Hollowdale felt like a place where they could just be kids again.

Lessons from Chapter 20: A New Beginning

1. **True strength comes from facing challenges together**: Emma and her friends learned that their strength came from working together to confront the magic and protect their town. In life, challenges are easier to face when we have support from others.
2. **Letting go of power requires wisdom**: The mayor clung to his magic, believing it was necessary to protect the town. Emma and her friends realized that true power lies in knowing when to let go and allow others to grow.
3. **Every ending is also a beginning**: Though the curse was broken and the mayor defeated, the group understood that this was not the end of their journey. In life, every challenge we overcome opens the door to new possibilities and responsibilities.
4. **Magic, like power, can be used for good or bad**: The group learned that magic itself is not inherently evil, but it can be dangerous if used for the wrong reasons. In life, the tools we use must be guided by wisdom and responsibility.

5. **Growth comes from adversity**: Emma and her friends had grown through their experiences, realizing that they could never truly return to the way things were before. Growth often comes through facing adversity and learning from it.

Chapter 21: Secrets Beneath the Town

The following days after the mayor's defeat brought a strange sense of calm to Hollowdale. People went about their daily routines, whispering about the strange events at the town hall, but none of them truly understood what had happened. To most of the townsfolk, the curse was just a story, a legend of the past that had finally been put to rest.

But for Emma and her friends, the reality of magic in their town was far from over.

Emma woke up one morning with a heavy sense of responsibility on her shoulders. The mayor had been removed from power, and the town was adjusting to the absence of his leadership, but the ancient magic that had once controlled the town still lingered. She couldn't shake the feeling that there was more to the magic of Hollowdale—something they hadn't yet uncovered.

When Emma met up with Liam, Noah, and Mia at their usual spot by the woods, the group shared the same unspoken concern. Though the mayor's magic had been taken from him, they all sensed that something deeper still remained hidden beneath the surface.

"So... what's next?" Mia asked, her voice filled with uncertainty as she glanced toward the dense forest that surrounded the town. "We stopped the mayor, but it doesn't feel like everything is back to normal."

Liam sighed, crossing his arms. "It's not. We've been focusing on the mayor's control over the curse, but I think there's something bigger happening. The magic we dealt with wasn't just about him—it's part of Hollowdale itself."

Emma nodded. "I've been thinking the same thing. The mayor said that the magic wouldn't disappear just because we stopped him, and I think he was right. There's still something powerful here—something that's been part of this town for a long time."

Noah raised an eyebrow. "But what do we do? We've already faced down wolves, a curse, and a power-hungry mayor. What could be left?"

Emma paused, her thoughts racing. "I don't know, but I think the answers are still here in Hollowdale. There's more history to this place than we've uncovered."

Mia frowned. "You mean like a hidden secret?"

Emma's gaze drifted toward the ground beneath their feet. "Exactly. Hollowdale's magic is ancient. It's tied to the land itself. If we want to understand it, we need to dig deeper—literally."

Liam tilted his head, his curiosity piqued. "What are you saying, Emma?"

"I think there's something hidden beneath the town," Emma said slowly, piecing her thoughts together. "The magic we've been dealing with—it's been focused on the surface, like the mayor's influence and the curse. But what if the real source of Hollowdale's magic is underground?"

Noah blinked. "Underground? Like... a secret chamber or something?"

Emma nodded, excitement bubbling up in her chest. "Exactly. The cave we found before—it wasn't just a random place. It was connected to the magic of the land. But what if there's something even deeper than that? A place where the magic originates from?"

Mia looked hesitant. "That sounds... kind of dangerous. I mean, we've already been through so much. Do we really need to go looking for more magic?"

Liam placed a reassuring hand on Mia's shoulder. "If there's something hidden, we need to find it. We've come this far, and we can't leave things unfinished."

Emma met her friends' gazes, her resolve firm. "We need to explore the land beneath Hollowdale. There could be something down there that explains why this town has always been connected to magic. And if we're going to protect Hollowdale, we need to know the truth."

With a plan in mind, the group set off to explore the town's outskirts, searching for any signs of underground tunnels or hidden chambers. They started by visiting the oldest part of Hollowdale, where the remnants of the town's early settlers still lingered—abandoned buildings, crumbling ruins, and forgotten structures that hinted at a past long buried.

It wasn't long before they found something.

Near the edge of the woods, hidden behind thick undergrowth and vines, they stumbled upon an old stone well. The well had clearly been unused for years, its stone walls weathered and cracked. But something about it caught Emma's attention—the faint glow of magic that seemed to pulse from the well's depths.

"There's something down there," Emma whispered, stepping closer to peer into the darkness below. "I can feel it."

Liam grabbed a flashlight from his backpack and shined it down into the well. The light barely penetrated the darkness, but they could see that the well was deeper than they had expected, with old stone steps leading downward into what looked like an underground passage.

"Are you sure about this?" Mia asked, her voice filled with apprehension. "It doesn't exactly look safe."

Noah grinned, though there was a hint of nervousness in his eyes. "Since when have we done anything safe?"

Emma smiled, her heart racing with a mix of excitement and fear. "We have to check it out. This could be the key to understanding the magic in Hollowdale."

One by one, they climbed down the stone steps, descending into the darkness of the well. The air grew cooler as they went deeper, the walls damp with moisture. As they reached the bottom, they found themselves standing in a narrow tunnel carved into the earth, its walls lined with ancient runes similar to the ones they had seen in the cave.

"This place is ancient," Liam said, running his fingers over the runes. "These markings are older than anything we've seen so far."

Emma nodded, her eyes scanning the tunnel ahead. "It's connected to the magic—just like we thought. We're on the right path."

They ventured further into the tunnel, the air growing thicker with the presence of magic. The deeper they went, the more they could feel the power of the land pulsing around them. It was as if the very earth was alive with energy, waiting for them to uncover its secrets.

After what felt like an eternity of walking, the tunnel opened up into a massive underground chamber. Emma's breath caught in her throat as she took in the sight before her—an enormous stone structure, like a temple, stood in the center of the chamber, its walls covered in glowing runes and symbols of power.

"This is it," Emma whispered, her voice filled with awe. "The source of Hollowdale's magic."

The chamber hummed with energy, the air alive with the presence of ancient power. As they stepped closer to the stone temple, Emma felt the pull of the magic growing stronger, drawing her toward it. She knew, without a doubt, that they had found what they were looking for.

But as they approached the temple, a low rumble echoed through the chamber, and the ground beneath their feet began to shake.

"What's happening?" Mia cried, her voice filled with fear.

Before anyone could answer, the runes on the temple's walls flared with bright, blinding light, and a deep, powerful voice filled the air.

"You have found the heart of the magic," the voice boomed, echoing through the chamber. "But to control it, you must prove yourselves worthy."

Emma's heart raced as the ground trembled beneath them, and the temple's runes glowed brighter.

They had uncovered the secrets beneath the town—but they weren't the only ones who had been waiting.

Lessons from Chapter 21: Secrets Beneath the Town

1. **The past often holds the key to the present**: Emma and her friends discovered that Hollowdale's magic was tied to something ancient and hidden beneath the town. In life,

understanding the past can help us make sense of the present.

2. **Curiosity leads to discovery, but also danger**: The group's decision to explore the underground tunnel led them to uncover the source of the magic, but it also brought them face to face with new dangers. In life, curiosity can lead to great discoveries, but it must be tempered with caution.

3. **Facing the unknown requires courage**: Venturing into the underground chamber took bravery, especially when they didn't know what they would find. In life, facing the unknown often requires courage and determination.

4. **Magic and power are not to be taken lightly**: The underground temple represented the true source of Hollowdale's magic, showing that power must be approached with respect and responsibility. In life, we must handle power carefully.

5. **There are always more layers to uncover**: Just when the group thought they had solved the mystery of the curse, they found a deeper source of magic. This teaches us that there is always more to learn and uncover in any situation.

Chapter 22: The Trials of the Temple

The ground trembled beneath their feet as the powerful voice echoed through the underground chamber, filling the air with ancient magic. Emma's heart raced as she stared at the glowing runes on the walls of the massive stone temple. They had uncovered the source of Hollowdale's magic, but now they were facing something far more dangerous than they had imagined.

"What does it mean, 'prove ourselves worthy'?" Mia asked, her voice shaking with fear as the temple's runes glowed brighter.

Liam glanced around, his eyes narrowed. "I don't think it's going to let us leave until we figure that out."

Emma took a deep breath, trying to steady herself as the ground continued to tremble. She had always known that the magic in Hollowdale was powerful, but this was different. This was ancient, raw magic—something that had been buried beneath the town for centuries, waiting to be awakened.

"We came here to understand the magic," Emma said, her voice determined despite the fear gnawing at her. "Now we have to face it."

Noah stepped forward, his eyes wide with awe as he looked at the temple. "But how? What does it want from us?"

Before anyone could answer, the rumbling beneath their feet grew stronger, and the floor of the chamber split apart, revealing three separate paths leading deeper into the earth. Each path was lined with glowing symbols, and each seemed to pulse with a different kind of energy.

"We have to choose," Emma said softly, her gaze shifting between the three paths. "Each path leads to a different trial."

Mia's eyes widened in panic. "A trial? What kind of trial?"

"The voice said we have to prove ourselves worthy," Liam reminded her. "I think each path is a test. We have to face whatever the temple throws at us."

Noah frowned, staring down each of the glowing paths. "But how do we know which one to take?"

Emma thought for a moment, feeling the pulse of the magic in the air. Each path seemed to be calling to them in a different way, like the magic was testing their instincts. She could feel the energy of the temple all around her, as though it was alive and watching them, waiting to see what they would do.

"We need to split up," Emma said finally, her voice steady. "There are three paths, and I think each of us has to take one."

Liam raised an eyebrow. "You sure about that?"

Emma nodded, though her heart was pounding. "It feels right. The magic is connected to all of us now. We've all been part of this journey, and we each have something to prove."

Mia looked uneasy but didn't argue. "Okay, but which path do we take?"

Emma stepped forward, her eyes scanning the three glowing paths. Each one seemed to pulse with a different color: the first path glowed with a soft green light, the second with a fiery red, and the third with a cool, calming blue.

"I'll take the first one," Emma said, feeling a strange pull toward the green path. "Liam, you take the second. Mia, you take the third."

Noah looked between them, his face pale with worry. "What about me?"

"You stay here," Emma said firmly. "Someone needs to keep watch in case anything happens. If things go wrong, we need you to be ready."

Noah hesitated, but he nodded. "Okay. But be careful."

Emma smiled, though her heart was racing with uncertainty. "We will."

Emma stepped onto the first path, the green light pulsing beneath her feet as she walked deeper into the temple. The air grew cooler as she descended, the sound of her footsteps echoing through the narrow tunnel. As she moved deeper into the earth, she felt the presence of the magic growing stronger, surrounding her like a living force.

After what felt like hours of walking, the tunnel opened up into a large chamber, and Emma stopped in her tracks. In the center of the room stood a large stone statue, its eyes glowing with the same green light that lined the walls. The statue held out its hands, and in its palms was a single glowing stone, pulsing with energy.

Emma's breath caught in her throat as she stepped closer to the statue. She could feel the magic radiating from the stone, but something about it felt... dangerous. It was as though the stone was testing her, waiting to see if she was worthy of taking its power.

"You've come to prove yourself," a voice echoed through the chamber, the same deep, powerful voice that had filled the temple earlier. "But are you worthy of the magic?"

Emma hesitated, her heart pounding. She had been through so much already—facing curses, wolves, and dark magic—but this was different. This was a test of her connection to the magic itself, a test of whether she truly understood the power she had been fighting against.

"I'm ready," Emma said softly, stepping closer to the statue. "I understand the magic now. It's not about control or power—it's about balance."

The statue's eyes glowed brighter, and the stone in its hands pulsed with energy. "You seek balance, but do you know what that truly means?"

Emma swallowed hard, her mind racing. "Balance means understanding both sides of the magic—its potential for good and its potential for harm. It means respecting the power, but not letting it control you."

The voice rumbled again, the statue's hands lowering slightly. "And what would you do with this magic, if you were to take it?"

Emma didn't hesitate. "I would protect the people I care about. I would use the magic to help, not to control."

For a moment, the chamber was silent, and Emma could feel the weight of the magic pressing down on her, testing her resolve. Then, slowly, the statue's hands lowered all the way, offering the glowing stone to her.

"You have passed the first trial," the voice said softly, as the stone's light dimmed. "The magic will follow you, but only if you continue to respect its power."

Emma took the stone, feeling its warmth in her hands. The moment she touched it, she felt a surge of energy flow through her, like the magic of the land was connecting with her on a deeper level.

She had passed the first trial.

Meanwhile, Liam stood at the entrance of the second path, staring down the fiery red tunnel before him. The heat radiating from the walls was intense, and he could feel the magic swirling in the air, thick with power.

"This is going to be interesting," Liam muttered to himself, stepping forward.

Lessons from Chapter 22: The Trials of the Temple

1. **Each person has their own path to follow**: The group's decision to split up and take different paths shows that everyone has their own unique journey to follow. In life, we each face different challenges that help shape who we are.
2. **Understanding power is more important than controlling it**: Emma's realization that magic is about balance, not control, teaches that true strength comes from understanding power and respecting its limits, not simply wielding it for control.
3. **Courage means facing the unknown**: Each member of the group had to face the unknown when they entered their respective paths. In life, courage is often about stepping into situations we don't fully understand, trusting ourselves to

handle whatever comes.

4. **Trials test more than just physical strength**: The trials of the temple are not just about physical power, but about wisdom, balance, and respect for the magic. In life, challenges often test our character, our values, and our ability to make the right decisions.

5. **Magic, like life, requires balance**: Emma's understanding of magic as a balance between good and harm teaches us that in life, we must find a balance in how we use our power and influence. With great power comes great responsibility.

Chapter 23: Liam's Trial by Fire

The tunnel opened into a massive chamber, and Liam stopped in his tracks, eyes wide. Before him was a pool of molten lava, bubbling and swirling in the center of the room. Above the pool, suspended in midair by glowing red chains, was a large stone pedestal. Resting on the pedestal was an orb, glowing bright red like a burning ember.

Liam felt the pull of the magic immediately. The heat radiating from the lava seemed to come from the orb itself, as if it were the source of the fire in the chamber.

"Fire is both a destroyer and a creator," a deep voice echoed through the chamber, the same voice that had guided them from the beginning. "It burns what stands in its way, but it also gives light and warmth. Do you seek its power, or do you seek to control it?"

Liam's throat was dry as he stared at the orb, the heat overwhelming. "I don't want to control it," he said, his voice rough. "I want to understand it."

The voice rumbled through the chamber, filling the air. "Understanding fire means understanding yourself. To master the fire, you must face your inner flame. Are you prepared to face your fear?"

Liam hesitated for a moment, feeling the weight of those words. Face his fear? He had been through so much already—facing wolves, dark magic, and powerful forces. But this felt different. This was personal. Whatever trial lay ahead, it was going to force him to confront something inside himself.

He took a deep breath and stepped forward.

The moment he moved closer to the pool of lava, the ground beneath him shook, and a massive wall of fire erupted from the pool, shooting up into the air like a burning wave. Liam jumped back, shielding his face from the heat, but the flames didn't reach him. Instead, they formed a barrier, blocking his path to the pedestal and the orb.

"This is your trial," the voice boomed. "You must cross the fire, but to do so, you must first understand what burns within you."

Liam stared at the wall of flames, his heart pounding. His fear, his doubts—they were rising to the surface, swirling in his mind like the fire in front of him. He had always been the one to act first, to rush into danger without thinking. He was the strong one, the one who fought to protect his friends. But now, in the face of this trial, he felt exposed.

What did it mean to face his inner flame?

As Liam stood there, staring into the fire, memories began to surface—memories of times when he had let his anger take control, times when his impatience had caused problems for the group. He remembered moments when he had acted recklessly, putting himself and others in danger because he hadn't taken the time to think things through.

The fire wasn't just about power. It was about control.

Liam clenched his fists, his heart heavy. He had always thought that being strong meant taking action, being the first to fight. But now, he realized that true strength came from knowing when to act—and when to hold back.

"I understand now," Liam said softly, stepping closer to the flames. "Fire can destroy, but it can also protect. I've let my anger and impatience control me, but I don't have to let that happen anymore. I can choose to control the fire inside me."

The flames flickered as if in response, and the wall of fire parted, revealing a path across the lava to the pedestal.

Liam's heart raced, but he didn't hesitate. He stepped onto the narrow stone path and made his way toward the pedestal, the heat from the lava still intense but no longer overwhelming. As he reached the pedestal, he reached out and grasped the glowing red orb.

The moment his fingers touched the orb, a surge of energy rushed through him, filling him with warmth and power. It wasn't the destructive heat he had expected—it was a steady, controlled fire, burning brightly within him but not consuming him.

"You have passed the trial of fire," the voice echoed softly, the flames in the chamber dimming. "You have learned that true strength comes not from controlling others, but from mastering yourself."

Liam held the orb in his hands, feeling the steady pulse of its magic. He had passed the trial, but more importantly, he had learned something about himself. The fire inside him was a part of who he was, but it didn't have to control him. He could choose to be stronger, not just in battle, but in how he handled the challenges life threw at him.

The path back to the entrance opened up, and Liam made his way out of the chamber, the red orb glowing softly in his hands. He knew that the trial wasn't just about magic—it was about personal growth, about facing the parts of himself that he had been afraid to confront.

Lessons from Chapter 23: Liam's Trial by Fire

1. **Strength comes from self-mastery, not control over others**: Liam's trial taught him that true strength isn't about controlling external forces or other people—it's about mastering his own emotions and reactions. In life, self-control is often the key to real power.

2. **Facing inner fears can lead to personal growth**: Liam had to confront his own anger and impatience, realizing that these traits could be destructive if left unchecked. In life, facing our inner fears and flaws is a vital part of growing as individuals.

3. **Fire symbolizes both destruction and protection**: The fire in Liam's trial represented both the destructive potential of anger and the protective power of control. In life, powerful forces like fire must be handled carefully to prevent harm and promote growth.

4. **Courage is in confronting ourselves**: Liam's trial wasn't just

about physical bravery—it was about the courage to look inward and face the parts of himself he had been avoiding. In life, true bravery often comes from confronting our inner challenges.

5. **Balance is key to using power responsibly**: Liam learned that power, like fire, must be balanced. In life, whether it's emotional, physical, or magical, power must be managed carefully to ensure it doesn't harm those around us.

Chapter 24: Mia's Trial of Water

Mia stood at the entrance of the cool blue-lit path, the soft glow of the tunnel calming her racing heart. But despite the calming presence of the light, Mia couldn't shake the sense of dread creeping up her spine. She had seen what Emma and Liam had already been through, and now, it was her turn. She wasn't sure what kind of trial the temple had in store for her, but she knew it would push her to confront something she had been avoiding for a long time.

Taking a deep breath, Mia stepped forward.

The tunnel was narrow and winding, with the walls lined in the same glowing blue runes that had illuminated the chamber. The further she walked, the colder the air became, as if the magic in the air was drawing all the warmth from the space around her. The sound of trickling water echoed in the distance, growing louder as she ventured deeper into the tunnel.

After what felt like an eternity of walking, the tunnel opened into a wide chamber. At the center of the room was a large, still pool of water, its surface perfectly smooth, reflecting the blue glow from the runes on the walls. Above the pool, suspended in the air by thin strands of water, was a glowing blue sphere—an orb similar to the one Liam had found in his trial.

Mia hesitated at the edge of the pool, staring at the orb. She could feel the pull of the magic in the water, just as Liam had felt the fire's heat in his trial. But the calmness of the water was deceptive. Mia knew that this trial was going to test her in ways she wasn't prepared for.

"You have entered the trial of water," a voice echoed through the chamber, the same deep, ancient voice that had guided them through the temple. "Water is life, but it is also depth and emotion. It can be gentle, but it can also overwhelm. To pass this trial, you must face your deepest fears, the ones you hide beneath the surface."

Mia swallowed hard, her pulse quickening. "My fears?"

"Yes," the voice rumbled. "The water reflects what lies within you. To take the power of the water, you must confront what you have kept hidden."

Mia's chest tightened. She had always been the quiet, cautious one of the group—the one who avoided danger, the one who preferred to stay in the background while others took the risks. But the truth was, her fears went much deeper than just avoiding conflict. There were things about herself she had been afraid to face, things she had buried deep beneath the surface.

Taking a deep breath, Mia stepped closer to the pool of water, staring at her reflection. For a moment, everything was still. Then, as she watched, the water began to ripple, and her reflection changed.

Mia gasped as her reflection shifted, turning into something unfamiliar. The face staring back at her wasn't just her own—it was a version of herself, twisted with fear and doubt. Her reflection's eyes were filled with uncertainty, and her expression was one of hesitation and insecurity.

"This is what you hide," the voice said softly. "You fear failure, weakness. You fear that you are not strong enough to face what lies ahead."

Mia's heart pounded in her chest. She had always known that she was afraid—afraid of making mistakes, afraid of not being as brave or strong as Emma, Liam, and Noah. But seeing it reflected back at her like this, so clearly and vividly, made her realize just how much her fear had controlled her.

"You must face this fear," the voice continued. "Only by embracing it can you move forward."

Mia clenched her fists, staring at her reflection. The fear that had been with her for so long—the fear of not being good enough—had always held her back. She had watched her friends face danger head-on, while she stood on the sidelines, too afraid to act. But now, she had no choice. If she wanted to pass this trial, she had to confront what had been buried inside her for so long.

Taking a deep breath, Mia spoke softly to her reflection. "I've always been afraid... afraid that I'm not strong enough, that I don't belong here. I've let that fear stop me from taking risks, from being brave."

Her reflection remained still, watching her with those same haunted eyes.

"But I'm done being afraid," Mia said, her voice growing stronger. "I know I'm not perfect, and I know I'll make mistakes. But that doesn't mean I'm weak. It doesn't mean I don't belong here. I've made it this far, haven't I?"

The water rippled again, and Mia's reflection began to change. The twisted, fearful version of herself slowly faded, replaced by her real reflection—calm, steady, and determined. Mia stared at her reflection, feeling a sense of peace wash over her. She wasn't fearless, but that was okay. Being brave wasn't about not feeling fear—it was about facing it anyway.

"You have faced your fear," the voice said softly, the tension in the room lifting. "You have shown that strength comes not from perfection, but from the willingness to confront what lies within."

The glowing blue orb above the pool lowered slowly, hovering just above Mia's hands. She reached out and grasped it gently, feeling a surge of cool energy flow through her, like the rush of water after a long drought. The power wasn't overwhelming—it was calming, steady, like a river flowing through her veins.

Lessons from Chapter 24: Mia's Trial of Water

1. **Facing your fears leads to growth**: Mia had to confront her deepest fears in order to pass the trial, showing that true growth comes from facing the things that scare us the most.
2. **Strength is not about being fearless**: Mia learned that being

strong doesn't mean never feeling fear—it means confronting it and moving forward despite it. In life, courage is about facing our fears head-on.

3. **Emotions are powerful, but they can be understood**: Water, like emotions, can be overwhelming, but it can also be calm and steady. Mia learned that by embracing her emotions, she could find strength in them.

4. **Self-doubt can hold us back**: Mia's fear of not being good enough had held her back for a long time, but by confronting that doubt, she was able to move forward. In life, self-doubt can keep us from reaching our full potential.

5. **Acceptance leads to peace**: Mia found peace by accepting her fears rather than running from them. In life, accepting our flaws and fears allows us to find balance and move forward with confidence.

Chapter 25: The Final Trial

Emma stood in front of the large, stone doors of the temple's final chamber, the green glow from the orb she had retrieved casting soft shadows on the walls around her. Her heart pounded in her chest as she prepared to face the last trial. She had seen what Liam and Mia had gone through—both had been forced to confront deep truths about themselves, truths they had been afraid to face. Now, it was her turn.

She knew that whatever lay ahead would push her to her limits.

Taking a deep breath, Emma stepped through the doors. The moment she entered, the air in the chamber shifted. It was different from the other trials. This room was vast, and in the center of the chamber was a massive tree—its branches reaching up to the ceiling, its leaves shimmering with an ethereal green glow. Roots twisted and spread out across the floor, pulsing with magic that connected to every part of the temple.

"This is the heart of the magic," Emma whispered, stepping closer to the tree. She could feel the power radiating from it, pulsing through the room like a heartbeat.

Suddenly, the ground beneath her feet trembled, and the same deep voice that had spoken throughout the temple echoed once more. "You have come to the final trial. You stand before the source of the magic, the heart that binds the power of the land to this temple. But before you can claim it, you must answer a single question."

Emma froze, her eyes wide as the voice filled the chamber. "What question?"

The voice rumbled through the air, filled with a solemn weight. "What will you do with the magic?"

Emma hesitated, the question echoing in her mind. It seemed so simple, but she knew it was more than just words. This was the essence of everything they had been through—the wolves, the curse, the trials. It all came down to how they would use the magic they had uncovered.

"I..." Emma began, but then paused, uncertain. She knew what the magic could do. It had been used for power, for control, for keeping the town under a spell of fear. But she also knew that magic wasn't inherently bad. It was the way it was used that made it dangerous.

"I don't want to control it," Emma said softly, thinking carefully about her words. "Magic isn't meant to be controlled. It's a part of the land, of nature, and it's meant to help, not to dominate."

The voice was silent for a moment, then spoke again, this time softer. "And what will you do to protect it?"

Emma swallowed hard, feeling the weight of responsibility settle over her. This was the heart of the magic that flowed through Hollowdale, and it was powerful—too powerful for any one person to control. The mayor had shown that. But if the magic wasn't protected, if it was left vulnerable, someone else could come along and use it for the wrong reasons again.

"I'll protect it," Emma said, her voice filled with determination. "Not by keeping it hidden, but by making sure that it's used wisely. The magic belongs to Hollowdale. It's part of this place, and it should be shared with the people, not kept for one person's power."

The tree's branches swayed gently, as though the magic within it was responding to her words. The pulsing of the roots seemed to slow, and Emma felt a deep sense of calm settle over the chamber.

"You understand the truth," the voice said, almost gently. "Magic is not about power or control—it is about connection. It is a gift, but it is also a responsibility. You have proven yourself worthy of that responsibility."

As the voice spoke, the roots of the tree began to shift, revealing a hidden pedestal at the base of the trunk. Resting on the pedestal was a final orb, glowing with a soft green light that pulsed in time with the heartbeat of the magic.

"This is the last piece of the magic," the voice said. "Take it, and with it, the power to protect Hollowdale."

Emma stepped forward, her heart pounding in her chest. As she reached out to take the orb, she felt the weight of everything that had led her to this moment—the journey, the trials, the responsibility of what lay ahead. But she knew that this was the right thing to do.

Her fingers brushed the surface of the orb, and the moment she touched it, a surge of energy rushed through her. It wasn't overwhelming like she had expected. Instead, it was calming, steady, like the pulse of the land itself. The magic flowed through her, connecting her to the earth, the trees, the rivers, and the people of Hollowdale.

It was a power that came with great responsibility, but Emma was ready.

"You have passed the final trial," the voice said softly, the air in the chamber growing still. "You are now the guardian of the magic. It is your duty to protect it, to ensure that it is used wisely and never for harm."

Emma nodded, holding the glowing green orb close to her chest. "I will."

As the room began to shift, the walls fading and the roots retracting, Emma found herself standing at the entrance of the temple once more. Liam, Mia, and Noah were there waiting for her, their faces filled with relief when they saw her step out of the chamber.

Emma glanced around at her friends, feeling the weight of the magic settle inside her. "We protect the town. We make sure that the magic is never used for harm again. But we don't hide it. We share it with the people—carefully, wisely."

The trials were over, but their journey had only just begun. Together, they would protect Hollowdale and ensure that the magic was used for good.

As they made their way back to the surface, the sun shining down on them for the first time since their journey began, Emma felt a sense of closure settle over her. They had faced their fears, passed the trials, and uncovered the truth about Hollowdale's magic.

And now, they were ready to begin a new chapter.

Lessons from Chapter 25: The Final Trial

1. **Power is a responsibility, not a right**: Emma's final trial showed her that magic isn't about control—it's a gift that comes with responsibility. In life, power should be used wisely and carefully, with consideration for others.

2. **Understanding comes from connection, not domination**: Emma realized that magic, like life, is about connection to the land, people, and the world around us. True understanding comes from respecting these connections, not trying to dominate them.

3. **Leadership is about sharing, not hoarding**: Emma's decision to share the magic with the people of Hollowdale rather than keeping it for herself teaches that good leaders use their power to uplift others, not to hoard it for personal gain.

4. **Courage is in accepting responsibility**: The final trial wasn't about physical bravery—it was about Emma accepting the responsibility of protecting the magic. In life, true courage comes from taking on responsibilities, even when they are difficult.

5. **The end of one journey marks the beginning of another**: Though the trials were over, Emma and her friends understood that their journey was just beginning. Life is a series of challenges and lessons, and each one leads to new opportunities for growth.